PAPER POPPIES

PAPER POPPIES

A Memoir

MARIANNA VEKHOVA

CLADACH
Publishing

Paper Poppies: A Memoir

translated from the russian by Natalia Klukovkina
original russian version published in moscow 2002

english version published with worldwide english rights by

Cladach Publishing
po box 336144
greeley, co 80633
www.cladach.com

printed in the united states of america

ISBN-13: 978-0-975961-91-9
ISBN-10: 0-975961-91-8

Library of Congress Control Number: 2005926708

To my prematurely deceased parents:
my mother,
who died in exile when she was twenty-three
and my father,
who was in the People's Volunteer Corps
when he was reported missing in action
near Rzhev at the age of thirty.

Preface

This book is the story of a spiritual journey. Much of it comes to us through the acute observations of a crippled orphan during World War II. Here described are the myriad of beliefs that filled empty souls during the Communist years.

Marianna's search for light begins on a dark night in a Siberian hospital ward and continues into adulthood. What to believe? How to discern Truth in the midst of a multitude of conflicting, cajoling voices?

Marianna chose to follow the faith of the first person who witnessed personally to her. Oh, the power of that personal word!

Marianna is still on her journey as are millions of Russians today, many of them orphans like Marianna.

For those who love Russia and seek to understand the struggle of the Russian soul, this book will allow you to enter that experience as no other.

When you purchase this book, you are contributing to the work of OPORA, an organization which mobilizes Russian churches to mentor children who are without parental care.

~ Pamela Brunson, World Witness, May 2005

One

We think it is wrong to talk to children about death. We think it is necessary to protect their psyches. As if children haven't witnessed wars and crimes from ancient times! As if they've never been taken captive and made to be slaves. As if all they've ever done was to play, sing and be merry.

My seven-year-old daughter and I stand by my grandmother's coffin, reading the funeral prayer. The child looks at the face of the dead woman without fear and says with a sigh as we finish the prayer, "It's good we didn't let her be taken to a hospital. It's good that she died at home with her family close. Look, she's smiling!"

My daughter knows how much I feared that Granny would die in a hospital—an alien and strange place—alone and feeling forsaken by the ones she loved. Never in her life had she been in a hospital.

I remember asking God, "Lord, when my Grandmother Eugenia's life is to end, let me be near her to close her eyes myself. Let her feel Your love." The longings of my heart were answered. In her last minutes Granny wasn't looking at us; she was gazing at an icon, immersed in prayer.

Death stood by my side even from my birth. Before my first birthday I'd undergone my first serious operation, trephination of the skull, because of neglected ear infections. Years of balancing between life and death followed. Something was dragging me into the darkness of non-existence. At the same time, something else was pushing me out of pain, oblivion and weakness into the colorful moving world full of joy.

There was no one to protect me from hard circumstances in my childhood. I could ponder death as much as I liked. I puzzled over its mystery.

At the age of five I first saw death close up. I was lying in a hospital in Sverdlovsk, Siberia. It was wartime. All hospitals and nursing homes were overcrowded, so the dying were no longer taken away to a separate ward as before, not even shielded with a folding screen from the others in the ward.

It sometimes happened that a dead woman would lie the whole night in her bed in the same ward with the living. Her body and head would simply be covered. Everyone would talk in a low hush. The ones who were allowed to get out of bed would walk noiselessly and would creep into the ward. Sometimes an especially brave one would come up to the dead, lift the sheet from her face and say, "Such a calm face, and peaceful. Must have been a good life she lived," meaning that she must have lived a praiseworthy and blameless life.

Others would turn away in fear. They were afraid of the spirit of the dead in that very room, complaining that now for sure she would haunt them at night. It was with great awe and wonder that I witnessed both fear and respect of death.

I wondered whether it was frightening to die. How would it be to see nothing at all, to hear nothing, to feel nothing? Why are a dead person's eyes often half open, as if they are peeping through their eyelashes? Why must one talk in whispers as if the dead can eavesdrop? Why are they treated differently from the living? The living are sworn at, shoved aside, and threatened. No one is afraid of hurting them but the dead are always approached with a look of utmost respect.

An old woman, speaking in a low voice, told me that the soul left the body like a butterfly leaves a matchbox. Flapping its wings, the soul soars up and lands on the Lord's palm if the person was good. The soul of a villain drops like a stone into hell, straight into the devil's black apron. With a horrible laughter, the devil stirs his hot fire with a poker, and there he will throw evil souls like pieces of black coal.

I imagined God sitting motionless on top of fluffy clouds, surrounded by blue, yellow, and patterned butterflies that danced over him as if he were an apple tree in blossom.

I didn't avoid thinking of death. Children don't have that cowardice of mind. They don't seek salvation in evasion. Instead, they feel on the verge of guessing a secret. Well-educated patients laughed at the old woman's imaginings of the immortal soul and said that to die meant simply to be no more. To them, that said it all. But I failed to imagine what it was like "to be no more," and listened with trepidation to the uneducated, old women's and nurses' talk of ghosts, dead people, and adventures at cemeteries.

I listened to these conversations all through the endless winter evenings in a hospital in a Siberian city in the middle of the war. Even now they remain engraved on my memory.

I would lie quietly like a mouse, trying not to breathe loudly, not to squeak the bed, fearing they would remember my presence and stop talking half-audibly in the darkness. Because electricity was rationed, the lamps in the hospital burned but dimly or the lights went out completely. Once in a while someone would light a candle on a bedside table, and then the knitters and embroiderers would move close to the little flame. Their shadows would quietly move against the walls and ceiling; peaceful, kind, not at all frightening.

Someone's face would emerge out of the darkness and vanish again. The candle would be flickering about with its sharp tongue and a gray tail of smoke. Behind the group of stooped figures, the windows shone with a thick coat of frost. The moon lit the frost, making luminescent blue and green spangles.

When the lights went out at night and the windows were uncovered, we could watch the moonlit night through those dark rectangles and wonder if ghosts in their long white shrouds were really freezing in the snow and wind while we were talking of them. Or perhaps they only tramped the Earth in old times, and now there's no such thing. I desperately tried to keep awake to catch a glimpse of a ghost peeping into our window. As much as I watched, I never caught one. I resisted slumber as long as I could. But I always fell asleep without having heard the end of the latest horror story.

In the daytime though, during the rest hour—called the 'dead hour'—I could ponder whether I would become a ghost after my death, or a butterfly, or a black stone. The idea of frightening people at night didn't appeal to me, nor did I want to drop into the oil-cloth apron of the devil, who had horns, a beard like a horse's tail, and a scorching fire. I wanted to swing up into the sky, racing with the wisps of smoke and clouds.

Two

I had turned five by then, but all I saw day after day were the whitewashed walls of the hospital ward, a patch of sky in the window, the nurses, doctors and fellow patients. I had spinal tuberculosis. I lay in a plaster cast tied to the bed with straps of cloth. The things around me were always the same: a plate, an aluminum spoon, and a white drinking cup with a straw. I learned to eat lying in bed with a plate on my chest without dropping a single crumb.

There was no opportunity for schooling or education. There was nothing to do. I escaped from boredom and idleness into my fancies and meditations.

With my face turned to the unevenly whitewashed wall, I could lie quietly as if asleep. But in fact, I was making up a story about a cockroach family that lived in a crack in the wall. The crack was barely noticeable, but even in broad daylight it was very dark inside. There was a cockroach that lived with his family in that darkness. He talked to his babies by touching their baby heads with his feelers, and they petted his cheeks with their feelers in return. Though they feared the light, they were very curious to take a look at it. Their father explained to them that they would learn all about the light in due course when they grew up. But they were bursting with desire to see some of it now, so they were secretly peeping through the crack and wondering. They had a lot of adventures. I made up sequel after sequel during dead hours, and these horrible hours passed away very quickly and were always alive for me.

This game ceased to entertain me when someone brought a book to one of the patients in my ward. It was Gogol's *Evenings On A Farm Near Dikanka*. Someone read the stories aloud, and every night as we listened to the prose, we shivered with horror and delight.

Surely our hospital dead were nothing compared to Gogol's ghostly characters. Ours looked like unimpressive shadows compared to his. On a dark night the spirits in Gogol's tales quietly flowed over tombs or empty roads, driving fear into the hearts of lone, night travelers. They appeared in dark cabins as quivering phantoms, or tapped at windows heralding someone's death. The worst thing was when they came in the form of a dead husband to his widow. But when the widow guessed the fraud and drew the sign of the cross, the dead (or the demon) disappeared with evil laughter.

Evil spirits of the lowest rank did petty mischief in cabins at night, just like naughty boys. They moved things about and stamped on the ceiling, leaving indelible footprints. They scratched, squeaked the doors, blew into peoples' faces, or howled, calling forth disaster. Sometimes demons would pour water over a frightened woman stiff with fear, alone in the darkness. Or they'd put a rake in front of a running man so he'd step on it, and it would suddenly hit him on the forehead. They'd drop a horse collar, that hung peacefully from a nail in the shed, on an old woman, who had crept out of the cabin in the middle of the night to answer the call of nature. But their main task was to frighten the poor traveler; to lead him astray in a blizzard, to lure him into a swamp or a pit—or worse, a forsaken tomb. Sometimes they entertained themselves by casting a spell over a maid or a newlywed woman.

Frightening, to be sure. But if you didn't give way to fear or depression, it was believed that you could draw the cross and drive away even the most cunning and evil demon. You could sprinkle him with holy water, invite a priest with a church crucifix, and have the house sanctified.

But none of us had ever heard of such monsters as Gogol's Basavrjuk or his sorcerer. What impressed me most of all was not dead men with claws growing down to the ground, with long hair and beards (Gogol's dead had hair that kept growing!). Of course it was horrifying to imagine corpses rising out of open tombs, their empty eye sockets peering at the moonlit river. But I was so terrified that I couldn't even breathe when we reached the chapter where a panic-stricken Katerina runs through the night forest, her hair catching in the branches, while souls of unbaptized babes laugh horribly and roll in stinging nettle. Oh, this stinging nettle! It spreads like a carpet, and a terrible squealing tangle of babes rolls over its pile.

And who was I? It turns out I was also a babe. One stops being a babe, they told me, when one turns seven, and I was only five. *Have I been baptized?* I questioned. *If I die, will I join the unbaptized babes? Why haven't I been baptized? Or perhaps Nanny did baptize me? No way do I want to roll and squeal in the nettles at night!*

When I was still able to walk, only one year before, I had seen trees and plants. And I had experienced stinging nettle. I'd been afraid my bare feet might be stung when we played hide and seek. I'd even eaten nettle soup. After a year in the hospital, though, my ideas of nettle and birches faded. The patients didn't have any nursery books with pictures. So the transparent blue soul of Katerina that came when called by the sorcerer was far more real to me than nettles.

THREE

The attitude toward life of the simple women in my ward was just like that of Gogol's. They believed that all kinds of beings existed in this world next to each other: people, mermaids, the spirit of the house (poltergeist), devils, and angels. For every human being—big, little, old, young, good or bad—there was a contest between angels and demons. Each person had a choice: to give into his passions and desires, thus falling under the power of the devil; or to resist his passions and desires and turn for help to his guardian angel, to the Lord himself, to a saint, or to an old and wise monk. Then rescue came immediately.

This worldview looked a lot richer and more interesting than did the cold, unpopulated world believed in by some of those in my ward. These were the people who kept arguing that neither God, angels, nor devils existed and that humans had no such thing as a soul. They had only a body with its liver, spleen, heart (its little engine), and brain (its head office). Anything that cannot be touched, weighed and scrutinized must be fiction!

I felt insulted, as if robbed, when the educated women won that argument. They said Gogol had imagined it all because he was a writer. Writers had nothing but fantasies in their heads and were not to be trusted. Death? It is when life snaps, just like a bandage or a thread. That is the end; there's nothing afterwards. Nothing!

The world according to Gogol and the simple-hearted women around me made sense. Man doesn't live his life just to finish up as worm food or as fertilizer for herbs. Man must master many things and learn about the next life that begins when the soul is departed from the body.

So easy to understand! Man is born little and weak, and he needs the care and labor of others to survive. When he grows up, he begins to labor for his children and other people, and he learns to love them. After his death, all these labors do not lose their value; but thanks to them, the soul lives on. Whether his soul will live in joy or in pain depends on his efforts in this life. It looked to me as if I paved the way for my future existence myself. Would it be a dash towards the sky, racing with the clouds, or a drop into the oilcloth apron of the monster in a horrible evil hell? God radiates love, but in hell there burns eternal hatred. It was so interesting to ponder this, that I stopped inventing my cockroach stories.

Now, as I lay in the hospital in my plaster cast, my back pain was not as bad as when I had lain on the floor in the cabin. I no longer cried constantly from attacks of pain. Most of the time, my back merely ached, sometimes badly, sometimes mildly. Still, when the weather was about to change, pain would start to gnaw at me and I would weep.

"I can teach you to drive away the pain if you wish," one of the patients whispered to me secretly.

If I wished! I wished it enormously!

"I'll teach you the secret words," she said. "Repeat them when it aches very badly and you'll feel better. But it will only help if you never tell these words to anyone. If you tell even one person, the words will lose their healing power."

She knew what would happen to her, should I let it out that she had taught me to pray. But so great was her kindness that it overcame fear. I was overjoyed that from now on I was going to have a secret of my own!

"Memorize it!" she whispered into my ear. "Our Father who art in heaven, hallowed be thy name ..." She taught me the entire prayer. "Memorize these words."

The words were so puzzling. Never had I heard words like that from anyone. I believed they were magical. Truly, they helped me survive the nights, when everyone was asleep in the ward, while horrible dreams wandered around the room, while the ache rose up and drove away sleep. One could discern groans and sighs of others tortured by their invisible pains. To me these pains had iron claws and huge teeth, red-hot from hell.

Yes, my pain feared the 'magic' words I kept repeating to myself through clenched teeth: "Our father who art in heaven ..."

My faith repeated the words while my mind pondered and wondered. *Why 'Our father' and not 'Papa?' And who is he? And why is he 'Ours?' Who is 'us?' Why 'thy' name and not 'your' name? And what is 'heaven'?*

In my imagination heaven looked like multi-tiered shelves of blue glass. Our Father sat on the top glass tier, cross-legged under a long garment, looking just like a Chinese figurine I had once seen on somebody's dresser. Our Father kept nodding his head and squinting his narrow, wise eyes. In his hands he was holding 'our daily bread'—a big loaf, white and crusty, with fried nuts on top. 'We' were a huge queue of adults and children who came up to the glass shelves and stretched out our palms towards him. Nodding and friendly, 'Our Father' would break off a large piece of bread for each one and put it into our palms. But the loaf of bread didn't get any smaller! The loaf remained complete and intact every time!

The woman who taught these secret words to me used to say that Our Father gave 'our daily bread' only to the good and turned his head away from the bad natured.

But if a bad-natured one is hungry, and he doesn't receive bread, he'll get angrier still and will take it away from the good, I thought. *And if he does receive bread, he'll eat it and will go on being wicked because there's no more bread left, and nothing is left over for tomorrow.*

I tried to find a solution to the problem of how to treat the wicked. I fell asleep quite confused, but pain tore me out of my slumber. So, once again I clutched the finger of Our Father, who tenderly nodded his head in the darkness. Strangely, when I was thinking of him, I was not at all afraid to be the only one awake among the sleeping; and I didn't feel lonely.

So, in our quiet ward we read Gogol's books, chatted together, and received our treatments. We hoped that one day we'd be released from the hospital and regain freedom.

Outside the hospital walls there continued a hungry, wartime winter. Everyone tried to feed us well and fatten us up, for we were TB patients, who were thought to need extra nutritious food. I remember one time when I turned down some kind of porridge. It was very likely the usual gruel that we had everyday. (The TB sick, especially bed patients, do not have much appetite.) The nurse was standing by my bed with a plate in her hands, trying to persuade me to eat.

"Do you hear?" the nurse warned. "A hungry woman is wailing over the radio, 'I want bread! I want porridge!' You hear? So, finish it up quickly, or she'll come and take it away from you!"

But I'd have gladly given my porridge to the woman wailing on the radio. ... The radio was always on in the ward. We eternally waited for any kind of news. A lot of patients felt oppressed by the quiet, and the radio distracted them and didn't let them concentrate on their misfortunes. I got used to the radio and came to love classical music, the arias from operas and musical comedies, and the folk songs. When the nurse frightened me with that hungry woman, the famous singer Ruslanova was singing over the radio. Her powerful voice drove depression into my soul. I felt as if I were about to suffocate from it and that my heart would stop.

Depression, worry, hopelessness and fatigue overwhelmed the sick women in my ward. They loved Ruslanova with a grateful love; they stopped talking as soon as they heard her start singing, and they listened with heads bowed. I liked what they liked. I trusted these women completely.

That mournful, emotional Russian music became associated in my imagination with endless stretches of snow. It always took me back to twilight over the snowy field, not a single light ahead, no hope to get warm or have something to eat. I had crossed a field like that somewhere in Siberia when the train with the sad whistle left me standing in a group of several women and children holding suitcases on the untrodden snow. The train disappeared into the gloaming. We huddled there together, and in every direction as far as the eye could see, there was nothing but endless, soft waves of white snow turning blue in the waning twilight.

When the train stopped to let us off, we were given directions to a village. But when we arrived at the village, the poor and hungry people there didn't welcome more mouths to feed. The grown-ups of our group felt confused, had a cry, and started to walk over a narrow path through the fields, exhausted under the weight of the heavy burden of suitcases and babes wrapped in blankets. We all were tiny, helpless beings alone in the silence of a huge, snowy world. There was no more rhythmic clatter of train wheels, no more snapping and crackling of the fire, no more talk, no more tears, no more walls that would protect us from the penetrating wind and the vast, endless emptiness that surrounded us.

I tried to walk in the deep tracks of the adults. Unfortunately the snow dropped into my boots from the walls of the footprints, and soon my feet were wet. It was hard to pull my legs out of the crumbling snowy impressions; my feet sank again and again. The night was falling fast, its invisible walls closing upon us. I wanted to drop to the ground and sleep, but it was too frightening to remain alone there where the wind wrestled with dry snow.

There was no more home—gone was my home, with its stone staircase leading to the first floor, and a high window overlooking the yard. The window opened right on the sandbox where I dug and built houses of wet sand. There was no more home with my cot, covered with a green blanket. No more one-eyed bear that always awaited me on my pillow. No more box of toys under the sofa. Now I wouldn't be afraid of the darkness under there. I'd pull out the box myself. I'd sit on the floor and play all alone. How was it that I used to fear the quiet in my room, the shadow in the corner, and someone's steps behind the door? I longed for even those things that once frightened me.

Nothing was left for me now. All I had was the squeak of snow under the heavy feet of the women and their loud labored breathing. Even the babies fell silent, and they whined no more. The squeak of snow moved farther and farther away from me. I had to run after the women, catch up and try not to fall or there would be no power to keep walking ...

In the hospital the sick women liked to sing. Their singing was the voice of their souls, of their bitterness.

When the day was over and the inky blue color filled the windows, the faces and other things in the ward turned gray. All became dim and sad. Someone would start a song in a low voice; there were tears in it already. When the song started to drown in the tears, at this point it was caught and carried further by other voices; and it would swing up, come back to life and circle long and tenderly under the ceiling painted dark-blue by the twilight. I would feel like crying aloud with the wailing of their singing. I wanted to join into the high-pitched, prolonged melody that spirited one away to some unknown place.

One song told the story of a coachman who lies dying in the snow of the steppe. With pain he thinks of his young wife. Then he curses his fate.

In the evening when darkness fell the singing ceased. Black blinds were quickly pulled down over the windows. Though we were far from the war front, it was mandatory to take precautions against enemy planes when we had lights on. A naked bulb hung suspended from a gray wire in the middle of the ceiling.

Then our 'fortune-teller' spread over a blanket her long-used, ragged playing cards with their gray edges. Quickly the spectators gathered round, forming a ragged queue. Every woman had a woe and wanted to know how much longer she'd have to bear it and what more to expect. Most of them worried about the fate of their loved ones at the front. The loved one usually was represented by the king of clubs or a jack. We were horrified to see the queen of spades next to the king or the jack, for the queen of spades meant death. If the ominous queen followed the king everywhere, the woman for whom the cards were laid was driven to tears. She was consoled and told that the cards often lied. Sometimes the cards were laid out up to three times for her. Still the worry sat on the unlucky woman's heart and wouldn't let go. Then, how impatiently she'd wait for tomorrow's fortune-telling!

These greasy, warped cards had such appeal. They were looked at with such hope. When they'd soften and forecast a long trip ahead or an important encounter in a state house, that was to be understood as "The regiment is moved to a different location" or "He's been called to the commander," perhaps to receive an award.

If the one for whom the cards were laid out was absolutely out of luck that day, and she started to weep, the fortune teller sternly told her, "Don't you cry! Don't call for disaster! Read the poem to God's Mama. She'll take away the disaster; the Patroness, she is." Then she recited in reverential silence:

The purest God's Mama, Mary—
Where have you slept and dreamt?
I slept and dreamt beyond the Lord's altar,
Under a white shroud;
I burned like an eternal candle.
I slept badly, I dreamt of many things:
Our Christ was being crucified,
A thorn crown put on his poor head,
His hands and feet pierced with nails.
Then went Mama Mary to the holy gates,
Weeping and crying.

Don't you cry, Mama Mary,
Your son's been on the crucifix for three days;
Bury him in the damp soil,
Drop your hot tears on him.
Then mother earth will open up,
And your Son will appear from his tomb,
Cast off his death shrouds,
And clasp his own mother in his arms.

It was believed that a big disaster was always heralded by signs. Certainly a crisis couldn't simply start all by itself without warning. The women constantly looked for signs and meanings to warn them. To support this superstition, each woman had a tale to tell. For example, one woman shared:

> *Listen to what happened at our place just before the war started. ... My elder brother was lying on the bed with his wife, resting. She fell asleep, and he looked up and saw a figure approaching him, someone furry, the face could not be seen. Came up to him, it did, and started to pet my brother, and petted, and petted. Brother couldn't restrain himself and asked, 'have you come to tell of good or evil?' The furry one stepped back and moaned, 'Of e-e-evil! Of e-e-evil!' And the war started the next day. Brother was drafted at once and reported missing in action. Where are his bones buried?*

Here's another woman's tale:

> *Our Pestrushka, such a smart chicken she was. She never laid her eggs anywhere but in the bushes. Mother had to hunt for them and cursed her. One day this Pestrushka flapped her wings, flew up and*

sat on the apple tree stump, and what do you think? She started to crow! Mother's face turned white. She clasped her heart and cried, 'Oh, something's sure to happen!' Just an hour later the woman who brings our mail said: 'War started!'

Years later, I wrote down these stories and tales. Here are the words of another woman who visited our ward:

Want to know why I hate war? War is war, but why were people tortured like that? I remember one woman, she ran to the mill seven kilometers away, to have her wheat ground into flour. Her five children waited at home. Suddenly a German car exploded nearby. They saw the woman run across the field and caught her and hanged her—not by the neck—just you imagine!—but by the jaw—so she'd suffer longer!

"Men fight, but why should children suffer?" someone responded. Many times I heard this question asked. Women would pat my head and give me lumps of rationed sugar, scraps of bandages, pill boxes, whatever they could spare. They believed the Lord immediately registered all kindly deeds and would repay them with kindness. This was believed to be especially true if one did a good turn to an orphan, for isn't the Lord the patron of orphans? One woman gave me her last piece of sugar, believing that someone would certainly give a present to her husband or son in return. Perhaps her generosity would make the bullet avoid her soldier son.

I became rich. I possessed boxes, bandages, and papers to play with. I had no scissors, so I learned to bite and tear the paper into dolls and dresses for them. I even made furniture from the paper and homes in empty boxes for my paper lodgers. I made beds and arranged them in rows to look like a ward. Little paper dolls were the patients. Scraps of bandages made the sheets, pillows, and blankets. Here the game ended. For what can happen to the patients? When they're all in their beds covered with blankets, what's next? The main events of the day are the doctor's rounds, treatments, and meals ... the same things every day.

It was a lot more interesting to play healthy people! They pay visits to each other. They go shopping. They dress up in frocks. They have children. Someone gave me some colorful and precious candy wrappers. These served as carpets and bed covers in my doll houses. My skill improved, and I produced more furniture for my dolls: sofas and easy chairs with lacy backs. The doors and windows in the houses could be opened and closed. The dolls could sit and look out the windows.

The sick women admired my work and gave me hundreds of new gifts. So it was that I learned from practice that one could master the pain of the soul if one made something that they, and others, would appreciate.

When I think back to my childhood, I can see clearly that it was the kindness of many people who came into my life that saved me. Though I was a lonely and sick child, I had no less love and care than does a child of the most loving parents. Often the love given to me was purer than a parent's love, for there was no egoism in it. Smiles lit up strangers' faces when they saw me. A sick person, who had not eaten enough himself, gave his best share of food to me. And his heart felt warmer from my joy and from his own hope that God saw everything.

Four

I had come to the hospital when war had at last receded from Moscow, and we who had been evacuated from the city started to return. Through a chance meeting on the street, Aunt Leah saw the woman who had taken me on the evacuation trip and who had abandoned me in the old woman's cabin. Leah then searched until she found me dying from bone TB, alone in a stranger's cabin in a village outside the city of Alapaevsk. She arranged my placement in the hospital. I don't remember that trip back to Moscow. But to this day I am haunted by memories of the earlier evacuation. ...

I could still walk at that time, and no one suspected that tuberculosis had started in my vertebrae.

The railway carriage was dark and overcrowded with worried people. It was not at all like the peaceful trains full of light we had traveled on when visiting our friends in the country before the war. On those Sunday trains one sang, rustled newspapers, and bought ice cream from women with carts. On top of these carts there stood boxes full of steaming dry ice. Tucked in the ice were pieces of chocolate in silver wrappers. Wafer cones with a thick rose of ice cream rested on top of the ice. One could tell they were sweet and stinging cold even from their looks. Children licked the ice cream and stared out open windows, while wind blew against their sweaty brows.

No, the evacuation train was different: saturated with fear that pressed down so heavily that even the children caught the general feeling of dread and sadness and didn't give any trouble. No lights were on. Red spots of cigarettes flew in the dark between the smokers' lips and their knees. The smokers inhaled and let their hands drop to their knees while a gray, wispy tail of smoke rose from their cigarettes.

We passed a train that had been bombed. It was burning still, blackened and abandoned. Our train didn't speed forward. It inched along, pressing its belly to the ground so that the bombers wouldn't notice it from high above. Everyone talked in half whispers and moved about cautiously. They tried to make it difficult for the enemy's invisible pilots who wanted to mix us with earth, to guess that we were here, so close and unprotected.

Even now I don't need to close my eyes in order to see that bombed train looking like a long animal with a broken spine. Its red sharp tongues of fire ran under the lifeless black cars and the heavy darkness of the sky, the sky that might hide our death as well. People sighed and said that those burning cars had also carried women, children, elderly, invalids, and wounded men.

The return to Moscow was not so gloomy, I'm told. The mood was even close to festive, because hope had come back to life. I don't remember anything in particular. I do wonder, though, whether they carried me in my plaster armor like a turtle dropped on its back?

The only thing I remember well is that I was not taken directly to the hospital from the train. My aunt had to pay many visits and go through many troubles before I was accepted at the sanatorium. I was lucky she was young, energetic and plucky.

In the meantime, I stayed with my Jewish Granny Brina in her dim apartment on Pechatnikov lane. Granny was very old and walked with much difficulty. Her eyesight was poor, but she was constantly busy running the house. She lived with her daughter and grandson in a small apartment packed with people. They occupied two rooms on opposite ends of the corridor of a communal apartment shared with three other families. All day long Granny scurried between her room where I lay, the communal kitchen, and the daughter's room at the other end of the long corridor. She never rested. I don't remember ever seeing her sit down to have a minute to herself. Her white head sailed through the corridor glowing in the dark as she passed by the open door into 'my' room. Her face turned to me, smiling with all its wrinkles. She tried to check on me as often as she could and even asked me to help her. Bursting with pride, I put the thread into the needle's eye and felt I was a great help. Unfortunately, I didn't know how to tie knots at the end of the thread, so Granny had to do that herself. Her fingers knew the process by heart, and she tried to teach me to do it.

"You see," Granny told everyone who came to visit, "she is my helper, my young eyes!" And they all praised me.

But not everyone was pleased with me. There was someone immensely irritated by my presence—my very handsome twelve-year-old cousin Andrei. Granny had given up her room for me. And now she, her daughter, and Andrei suffered from being crammed together in the other room.

I was extremely nasty to him. He stayed away from me, and I wanted to draw his attention to myself. He had nothing to talk to me about. I noticed long ago that sick, unhappy, or crippled people often seem repulsive to healthy people. This feeling was often mingled with fear as if any disease, any suffering was contagious and could be caught by the healthy.

I saw this familiar disgust reflected on Andrei's face. It concealed itself and slipped out often against his will, making my heart shrink with pain. Now I know his reaction was natural. A child can more easily feel sympathy for a sick kitten or an injured baby bird than for people who are suffering, when they could easily be the ones suffering.

But, all the same, I was burning with desire to revenge myself for his neglect. I chose the form of revenge that was the most painful for him.

Our radio hung on the wall above my head. It looked like a black plate, similar to the ones in every Russian home at that time. To cover their bareness, the radios were often draped with a lace cloth, which shivered with the vibrations of sound.

We all waited eagerly for the war news but were most eager for one particular radio broadcast. Each evening we heard the introduction that sounded like glass beads dropping, followed by the first phrase of the song "My Country is Wide"; then, after a pause, more beads, and the song again, it was time for the evening news.

Immediately stopping whatever he was doing, Andrei would rush to the radio. He would raise his anxious face towards the dish. What city have we fought in and won back today? Will there be fireworks to celebrate?

I saw my chance to show the arrogant boy that I was worth noticing even though I was sick. At the sound of the last call, before the first words of the famous and solemn-voiced broadcaster began ... I "turned on the siren." I screeched in the nastiest and the most annoying way imaginable, wailing at the top of my lungs to drown out the speech of the announcer.

Poor Andrei gave a start of indignation and waved his hands at me. His handsome black brows over his dark velvet eyes frowned menacingly. Even his hair seemed to stand up on his head in protest, but I only increased the howl. Andrei then grabbed a stool and mounted it to be closer to the radio. He was ready to dive into the black dish. He would have gladly thrashed me. But one could not thrash a suffering, plaster-clad child, even if she was nasty and obnoxious. A sick child indeed!

I triumphed in my victory of seeing Andrei boiling with rage as he balanced on tiptoes on the stool under the radio. I only felt sorry I couldn't knock him off this stool with my shouting, just as boys knock a sparrow off the fence with a stone. But in the evening he would run off to watch the fireworks. How much I wanted to see them! I would hear shouts of "Hurray" and laughing voices from the street. The cannons boomed nearby in Red Square, but I saw only a green glare on my window, then yellow or red. Then the color faded till cloudy wisps gradually floated away and vanished through the sky.

What city it was that had been liberated I didn't care to know. War ... other cities ... as much as I heard people talk of them, they were not real to me. To a small child, the only real things are the ones that happen to her, only what she sees with her own eyes ... or perhaps the things she fancies. Sometimes these fancied things are even more real. Anything else, what takes place somewhere far away, or even outside the home, is just unimaginable.

Andrei had an active life completely unknown to me. It was somewhere outdoors. Sometimes his friends came to visit. I heard their voices and footsteps. I saw their figures move through the corridor, and they seemed mysterious.

Then there was Granny's cat, Smoke. He disdained the entire human race and looked down on it from his throne, a large chest. I first saw him when I was being brought into the apartment. I thought it was someone's fluffy fur collar lying on the chest. But I was told, "Look—this is Smoke, our cat."

What proud manners he had! The king of cats he was; a Siberian cat with a fluffy coat. He really was like a cloud of smoke billowing upwards on a frosty day from the chimney of a country house. Fluffy and long, he had a mysterious glint in his eyes, as if he knew some secret hidden from people. I was dying to touch his smoky fur and take a close look at his large whiskers, ears, and eyes. But he was as inaccessible as Andrei and sometimes he glided like a gray shadow past my open door and disappeared in the dark depths of the apartment. I had no power over him and could in no way attract his attention.

But I was loved by Granny Brina! What a lovely face she had, with regular features and a cloud of white hair over the tanned forehead. I heard she had been a wonderful beauty in her younger years: gray-eyed, with ashen hair reaching her heels. Her husband wouldn't let her cut her braids, and maintaining such long hair was a great deal of work in her busy life.

Her arranged marriage to the owner of a linen shop in the town of Berdichev had occurred when she was only fifteen years old. Granny Brina gave birth to ten children, all of whom she raised to adulthood.

Her husband knew what he wanted out of life and out of people. When I hear the word "businessman," I immediately think of Granddad Mark. He was overflowing with business energy. He was so full of ideas and plans that they didn't let him live peacefully. He was a concentrated force. But the revolution stripped his life of meaning. There were no more private businesses or businessmen. In the passivity that followed, he couldn't survive and started to deteriorate.

I felt Granny Brina's love physically; just like one feels the warmth of the sun, the comfort of a warm radiator or kitchen stove. I was afraid of losing her favor. Her coming into my life, and her kind smile, were enough to cure my tantrums. She drove away the black moods and hysteria that I would get into to protect myself and fight against those I didn't want to obey. It was she who helped me, in a later era of my life, to understand the meaning of "the fear of God." For me it was simply the fear of losing The One who is very dear.

Five

During a month of lonely solitude at Granny Brina's, I lay listening to the radio. There were often piano concerts that reminded me of something that had happened in my life a long time before. ...

Had it been myself or not, that little three-year-old girl, under the grand piano, between its dusty, curved legs? The piano had stood so firmly on those legs. I liked to crawl under and imagine that it was my own palace with columns. It had been my aunt who played the grand piano. Her embroidered skirt with hem-stitching shook and swayed each time her leg would energetically press the pedal. The piano would rumble above my head, and the floor would shake and vibrate.

Papa would bend down to look into my rumbling palace and laugh. His white teeth shone. His face, turned upside down, seemed so very funny to me. His glasses would drop from his nose to the floor. He'd gasp, stretch out a hand to catch them and crawl under the grand piano to hunt for them. I wouldn't give him back his glasses, for it was so nice to see him under the piano. It was as if he turned little just like me and came here to play with me. ...

Thoughts of Papa made me want to grow up, be healed, and

then go to seek the battlefield where he had died. I thought, *I'll find it! I'll surely find it! I'll bring him back to life! I'll bring all the warriors on that field to life!* I imagined myself as a grown-up: beautiful in a Russian jumper and embroidered blouse, a thick plait of golden hair tied around my head. ...

> *In my dream I see myself walking slowly across a battlefield. It is huge. It stretches from one horizon to the other. Big black birds circle over the field. In the trampled grass dead soldiers lie, their arms thrust wide apart, and their open dead eyes peering into the sky. I lean over them and look into each still face. But I don't see any face I know. I straighten up and look around the field. How many people died here!*
>
> *I ask them, 'What did you die for?'*
>
> *'For the Motherland,' vague, heavy voices answer.*
>
> *I pick up a handful of soil. It is dry. It turns to dust in my hand. It is scattered by the wind. Far away, at the edge of the field a mighty oak tree spreads a wide shadow on the grass. I step into its shade. There I see my father lying under the oak tree.*
>
> *He's lying there, not breathing. His face looks like he's asleep. The wind is playing through his hair. I gaze at him and weep.*
>
> *I kneel next to my father. I look into his face, white as a hospital sheet, motionless, dead, fallen back towards the sky, and I shout out loud, 'For whose sake have you forsaken me?'*

A baby raven, a live black shadow, lands on my shoulder. I take from its beak a vial filled with the water of life. I sprinkle the water on my father's dead face.

He opens his eyes. 'Oh, I slept so long. I slept—'

'You'd have slept longer but for the water of life.'

'How much you've grown!' he exclaims.

We walk across the battlefield and bring all the dead back to life. Silvery seeds of the water of life drop from our fingers. The huge field begins to move, to sigh, even the grass whispers, 'How long I slept ... long ... long. I slept ... slept ...'

The soldiers shake the soil off their clothes and cast off their helmets, all rusty from rains, snows, and blood. People wake and walk. They drop the rifles necessary no more, the horrible-looking gas masks with elephant trunks, the spears, the shields, and the swords.

Many years later, when I was a student, I visited the Smolensk battlegrounds—a marsh in the middle of a withered and sick wood, where water squished under one's feet, water saturated with ashes—dead water. Wet bones broke and crumbled in one's hands. On one knoll there was a row of skulls with horrible, lacerated holes. Some of the skulls one could barely extract from the helmets. What misery and bitterness soaked every tree limb and drop of water.

I've been to another battlefield. It was on the high bank of the Dnepr River. The soil between the tufts of grass was so dry it was like walking on stone all covered with cracks. It reminded one of a sick, scab-covered hand. From the road the field looked even and smooth. It was in fact a chaos of grass-filled craters, trenches, ditches, knolls, and bumps; and everywhere hairy plant stems swayed before my face. Prickly seeds and heavy thistle leaves blew in the dry wind, and branches caught at my clothes.

Climbing the knolls that crumbled under my feet, I watched the sunset gradually spread over the entire sky. It was so fiercely crimson that I felt uneasy. The sunset was raging, as if a wooden city was on fire beyond the field. All of a sudden a flock of ravens took off with a loud noise. They were like the black soot of a fire. The whistling of their many wings sounded like rusted voices.

The quietness—hot and forlorn—dropped over me again. I stopped, looked around, and realized where my fear came from, why it oppressed me so much on that ancient land. How much blood must have been shed there! Every particle of that dry clay was likely mingled with human ashes.

Maybe my ancestors, concealing themselves in that place, had also looked to where the earth was joined with the sky. Were they waiting to see if the earth would shudder, and black horsemen would ride out from behind the horizon? With a shriek and a clatter of hoofs they would fly at you. There'd be no way out. You'd try to chop, slaughter, and beat off, while you were suffocating. You'd drop just under the hoofs of the snorting horses, be drowned in pain, blood, and mortal fear. With your last glance did you follow a bird shadow in the sky or stare at a thorn at the end of a swaying leaf? You'd dissolve in the dry soil or in the grass. What does the soul feel, so swiftly and prematurely parted from the body? Does it fly somewhere? Fall asleep? Drop into unconscious torments?

Their voices, their breath, their fury—they've all disappeared, just like water disappears into the sand. Under which hill is my father lying? Would he recognize my steps? He'd not be able to tell them from the steps of others. I've become a different girl than the one he knew. To him I'm still the child who could fit into his arms, who had to be protected from everything: from a cold, a cough, a nightmare, war.

Neither would I be able to look at my father with the eyes he loved so much. My eyes have changed, and his face has moved somewhere so far away that even its outline is blurred. His face started to fade from my memory a year after our parting. It mingled with the face of every kind man I met....

The first of these encounters with kindness was in Siberia during the evacuation. The tuberculosis was destroying my spine. I could only walk with my back bent, and leaning heavily against my knees with both hands. I was very weak and tortured by pain. It was exhausting, incessant, sometimes aching; but more often it was like burning explosions inside my bones. During the worst attacks, I no longer shouted or cried. I screamed, not hearing my own voice, just feeling my throat grow sore and raw.

I looked for some way to distract myself from the unbearably acute pain and found it, in another pain. I bit my hands. My teeth were sharp and left deep wounds. Hot blood ran from them. As a result, I was bound hand and foot. I couldn't lie on a bed, only on an even, hard floor. So I was put on the floor on a blanket. It was over this blanket I rolled with my hands tied, exhausted from pain and fever. For on top of tuberculosis I was ravaged by malaria.

I was in such a state when I found shelter at an old woman's cabin. She was poor and had no family. I don't know whether my wails drove her away from home, or whether she worked somewhere, but she left me alone in the cabin for the entire day.

Once I was shouting, crying, rolling on the floor, shaking from cold when I suddenly saw a man—a soldier—next to me on the floor. His white face seemed to glow in the dark. He sat there and held my hand. He caressed my hair, my forehead, my cheeks—stroking very lightly even though his hand was big and heavy. He told me a long story to distract me from the pain. I asked him to find my papa at the war and beg him to come to me as soon as possible. I believed that, should Papa only come, my pain would go away immediately and all would be as before: Moscow and kindergarten, where we had cocoa with a bun for breakfast. And in the evening I would sit under the table at home, concealed by the long tablecloth, and play house with my dolls.

Later I learned from the women who were in evacuation with me that the soldier who held my hand and seemed to me a real grown-up uncle was a very young lieutenant, who must have just graduated from the military college. Walking by our cabin, he heard my screams. He thought someone was torturing a child inside. Somehow he got into the house and stayed with me as long as he could. He left his rations for me: butter, sugar, canned meat, cereal ... and then he had to leave. He disappeared forever.

The old woman, my benefactress, said: "Ah, the Lord sent you an angel. The Lord doesn't forsake orphans."

It gets dark early in Siberia in winter. We kept a candle burning. The landlady would come at night, when I, having scraped up enough strength for shouting and crying, woke her. She suddenly appeared from I don't know where. Holding a candle, she stood tall in something long and white, with her long gray braided hair lying on her bosom.

She tried to reason with me. "Are you crazy, girl? You'll ruin your voice, and then how will you sing?"

Or sometimes she frightened me. "If you go on yelling like this, the witch Baba Yaga will hear you and come and devour you."

"She won't," I replied with assurance. "I take quinine! My flesh is bitter. She'll bite off a piece and spit it out."

"Bite off a piece, yes! And it will hurt! Her teeth are like huge saws."

Taking quinine made even water taste bitter. The very air I inhaled seemed bitter. Even fever feared this bitterness and stopped shaking me in the evening.

Every night the tiny light of the candle did battle with the huge shadows that gathered around me. It seemed to me those shadows were my pain. For a long time afterwards, I was afraid of night shadows! They wanted to tear me apart. They stretched their long arms toward me. They moved noiselessly and mysteriously from one place to another. Only when someone came to me and took my hand, did the shadows shrink away in fear. Then even the pain faded.

When the soldier came with his firm and manly face, then the shadows shied away completely. It seemed to me they pretended to be kind and started a round dance on the walls and ceiling. The pain almost disappeared, and I could at last get enough sleep.

I fell asleep and woke up again, and he still was sitting there holding my little hand in his large and rough hand. Tears rolled from his eyes when I reached up to lightly pat his cheek. I seemed to enter his world without leaving mine, and started to feel for two, for myself and for him. I had a high fever. I was burning, my skin ached all over my body, and my muscles were filled with dry fire, and the pain in the spine came and went in fits. My feverish hand touched his cheek lightly, brushing it with the fever.

His cheek was prickly like that of my Papa's, who had vanished somewhere and couldn't come to me. Crowds of worried and tired people, rumbling railway cars, frost, snow, darkness behind the window, darkness inside a stranger's house, and pain in sleep and in waking—all came between us and separated us forever.

My pain and fears overflowed into this young man who was called to my side by pity. He has remained forever in my memory. Perhaps it's only in my memory that he's alive now? Or was it really the Lord's angel?

The angel had a prickly cheek. That means they also shave in Paradise, I was thinking to myself when the old woman who owned the house explained to me who angels were, where they lived and how they treated us people. But how did the Lord's angel learn about me and fly to me with gifts? He put on a field shirt, so as not to be recognized. That's easy to understand. But if he's an angel, he'll find my Papa at the front. He'll tell him I'm sick. And Papa will come.

In January 1942 Papa wrote to his mother-in-law, my grandmother Zhenia: "Last month has been very difficult for me, even now I can not quite become myself again." He found it hard at war, though he'd gone many times before on science expeditions to the mountains and to the desert.

Now I can easily imagine what December and January, with their frosts and winds, were like in dugouts and trenches. You could not warm up or get dry. You faced constantly soaked shoes and wet greatcoats, a mixture of soil and snow under your feet, fingers unbending from frost, and frost-bitten cheeks. There was constant pressure and strain. It seemed as if the incessant frost had frozen everything inside you: thoughts, knowledge, dreams, and all desires but one—to get warm and sleep in a warm place.

Later I experienced these feelings firsthand when, in my student years, I joined a multi-kilometer ski hike across the forests of Bryansk. I wanted to test myself for survivability and stupidly hadn't thought that I might turn out to be a burden for the others. I concealed from them that I had had spinal TB. Thank God, all turned out well.

But within half an hour, my ski boots became wet. Two hours later, water was squelching in them. If I stopped, I started to freeze, my underclothing got wet, and the wind seemed to whip right through me. I felt better by the fire, but my face burned, my mittens steamed, my back was bitten by frost. I thought that this must be what our soldiers, surrounded by these same forests in winter, had felt. Since the edges of the wood could have been mined with explosives—a snowy hill, a forlorn lodge, a tree-lined road—every place may threaten with death. It was dangerous to light a fire, or to enter a peasant house that smelled of fur coats warmed on the furnace. Where could one safely step? Who could one trust?

We tourists were lucky! It was a small thing if the boots were soaked, hands were cold, the backpack got heavier and heavier, and our feet could barely move. These were just for the moment. We had a merry supper waiting for us in a house well heated by the fire, with talking and maybe even dancing. There wasn't any need to hurry. Was it important if we made this distance not in seven days, but in eight? We had a large stock of cereals, canned food, and in a village one could buy a chicken and have a feast. It was merry to watch the darkness concentrate in the forest under fir trees, to watch the snow turn blue, the crescent moon light up in the sky, and the stars shyly start to burn against a still sky....

My father must have looked up, perhaps from a wet pit, at the stars so well known to him as an astronomer. Was he exhausted, with no hope of remaining alive? The speedily-dug shelters didn't shield from anything, not even an illusion of protection did they give. Everything that made up his life before must have started to lose its meaning. As early as November 1941 he wrote to his mother-in-law, my Granny Zhenia: "Take the girl to live with you, bring her up, and tell her the truth about her mother and father." He knew that he would never tell me anything himself.

Six

When I at last arrived at the Moscow sanatorium, a nurse brought me into a ward full of children. All the heads on the beds turned my way, and many voices asked simultaneously: "Girl, what is your name?" I loudly gave my name at the same time as the nurse: "Marianna! Marianna!" My name flew around the ward, and I felt glad I had such a beautiful name.

The ward was full of light and seemed huge to me. The children were holding real toys, not like the paper ones I had made. There were colorful books, and in the space between two windows there stood a self-important black piano. I felt glad. It seemed to me that this was the beginning of a happier childhood.

During those years of war, one of the first questions children asked each other when they met was "Where is your Dad?" How hurt the ones felt who could not proudly answer, "At the front, of course!" Because the next sentence of the new acquaintance was "My father is at the front! He's an officer!" I was glad I could answer with dignity, "My father is also at the front! He's also an officer!"

As five- or six-year-old children, for some reason we felt that the officers faced the most risk. We felt that war must be easier for common soldiers. Children felt ashamed to say that their fathers were just soldiers. Everyone wanted to surround his father with a halo of glory. So everyone imagined his father was somebody's commander. The clever ones boasted that their fathers were scouts or belonged to the tank corps. Children of aviators were envied most of all. The lucky ones whose fathers were in the cavalry were considered heroes. It was as if it were they and not their fathers who rode on fiery, hot-blooded horses, brandishing a sword over a pile of the defeated enemy. The foes were scattered like rag dolls. Blood, wounds, screams, groans, sweat, dirt—all those things did not come into our imaginings. In the movies the wounded were neatly bandaged and dragged back to their camp by beautiful, strong, heroic nurses.

Our ideas of the front were as romantic and picturesque as a postcard. Later, in high school, I wrote:

Our fathers come to us in our dreams
With sharp swords and of course on horse back,
And of course they are giants and champions!
(Where are their bald spots and glasses?)
And of course they rush as hurricanes
Charging at the cowardly and stupid enemy.

How easily we children glorified ourselves! We earned prestige for ourselves by the sufferings of our fathers. We kept boasting of the heroic deeds we imagined for them and didn't even suspect what they felt in reality.

We were just as ignorant of our own tragic situations. We simply lived day after day. We played. We quarreled. We cried from hurt feelings or from pain. We learned. We fancied. We chatted. We did all these things as we lived tied to our beds and didn't feel much of a loss in our situation. We didn't think of our future as hunchbacks or cripples, or with paralyzed legs.

A child is so focused on the present, that the future does

not exist for him. It may appear suddenly sometime in a tempting fancy, but it is as abstract to the child as life after death is to adults busy with their own affairs. Of course, all children want to grow up as soon as possible and turn into adults, to be strong and independent. But what it really means to be grown up, they have no idea.

I lived in my white bed in the ward. A large pocket for toys was tied on one of the bedposts. I could pass my hand between the rods of the back and get a small toy. If I wanted a larger one I had to ask a nurse for that doll or teddy bear or book. Bonds safely tied me to the bed so that I couldn't jump and put an additional load on my damaged spine. From armpits to knees I was in a plaster cast. My shoulders were pressed to the hard mattress with "bagels"—soft cotton ropes equipped with firm straps tied to the bed frame. The plaster cast was also tied to the frame, and I was laced up like a boot with long cords in a fabric corset together with my plaster. Bagels tied my legs to the bed by the knees and the ankles. I was free to turn my head right and left, but I wasn't allowed to have a pillow. The pillows were only for the lucky ones who had TB of the joints.

We were greatly afraid of dropping anything. We made up a saying, "Whatever has fallen is gone." A nurse would come and sweep the dropped thing into the trash, because there were plenty of harmful germs on the floor. Our floor was always polished so that it shone, but that didn't change the belief that it was swarming with germs. One could not take back to bed what had been on the floor. The germs would spring from the dropped thing onto your hands and from your hands into your mouth and from the mouth into your tummy. And you would have to get shots for some dangerous disease.

We became skillful at tossing little objects and treats from bed to bed. We had to aim perfectly and toss them so that they would land right into the waiting hands or on the blanket by the chest—certainly not farther than the hips, for if the parcel dropped on the legs we could not get it without torments.

Possibly the blanket could be pulled up, but then how was it to be pulled back down? The feet were bound to stick out naked. If the thing dropped to the floor altogether, we might weep for the bad luck. There was nothing to do but appeal to the mercy of the one who was closest to the parcel, if he could pick it up, and promise him something for his work.

First we had to estimate whether the dropped thing was within someone's reach. If so, it was necessary for them to scoot to the very edge of the bed and stretch all the way out like a worm. Then the enterprising nearest one would secretly but swiftly start to get out of his bonds under the blanket. Neither doctors nor nurses could imagine how fast and how skillfully most of us could undo all those tricky knots. They thought it impossible without outside help!

At last the freed one would stretch and stretch and lean over, risking a fall to the floor. His body was suspended in the air, till eventually he'd reach with spread fingers the dropped thing and grab it. Hurray! All the spectators would give a sigh of relief and start to smile and chat excitedly, discussing the minute details of the event and praising the adroit "getter." He was looked at with respect and paid approving glances and exclamations.

Sometimes I would pull the sheet over my head. Then I was alone in a white sarcophagus. I could dream, I could muse and scrutinize Daddy's photo.

When I think back on my hospital life in Moscow, I remember it as a row of light and merry days. In my memory it was never gloomy in those years. I don't remember the cold, damp, or dark, but a long and warm summer sun that seemed to shine all the time.

In the summer we lay on a glassed-in veranda and watched the wind romping in the tousled tree tops, brushing them as if they were heads of hair. We watched the birds alighting on the branches from the blue sky and grasping the limbs with their claws as they swung in the breeze and then vanished again into the sky. Heavy and tired bumblebees plopped onto our blankets. We examined them as we held our breath with fear of their stingers. A bumblebee, waddling like a bear, would creep through the folds of the blanket. He seemed to puff and steam in his coat of long orange fur. A strong gust of wind rolled, swishing green waves over the tree tops. Patches of sunlight crossed our blankets, shining on the folds and were put out again in a moment by little round shadows of leaves.

It was so good on the veranda in summer!

The nights were also wonderful and quiet. The trees all around seemed warm and satisfied. They were glad that the day had passed so happily and they believed that all would be well tomorrow, too. The darkness and the quiet settled slowly. Occasionally, baby birds in their nests chirped something sleepily and their mothers drowsily replied. We talked in whispers, slowly falling asleep. Our best friends were very close. We could hold hands, turn faces to each other and chat in whispers. It was a joy to feel a special trust and tenderness, to be listened to, to be admitted into somebody else's world that was otherwise locked to all strangers.

I remember how we, three girls of seven years, talked of how many children we would have. We asked the night nurse if we would be able to have children. She replied that we surely would. We dreamed of how we'd name them, what clothes they'd have, what color hair and eyes they'd have, and how we'd play with them. We looked into the darkness of the night with eyes open wide. You had to struggle so as not to drop asleep right in the middle of a most interesting conversation.

Buried deeper in my memories, though, is the realization that not everything was happiness and light. Our childhood friendships were sometimes marred by our pride, envy, ambition, vindictiveness, and even hatred. It was just as happens between normal sinful people who had not been taught to take into account the dignity of fellow creatures.

It's harder to be a child than to be an adult. Children openly assert themselves at the expense of each other. This is especially true of sick and lonely children, overstrained, nervous, and left to their own devices. Dark passions writhe in such children's collectives, restrained by nothing except force or fear of punishment.

Fortunately, children's evil passions (as well as their good feelings) are short-lived and not deep. Burning hatred may turn into passionate friendship. A seemingly strong friendship may burst and drown in a squabble or from ridicule. Children practice all their feelings on one another. They try different variants of any relationship.

I moved from an adult society into a world of children, and this turned out to be quite an ordeal. With the grown-ups I was the center of attention, the object of their kindly and tender feelings. Grown-ups spoiled me with their kindness. Among themselves they also quarreled a lot less than did the children. They were ashamed to wrangle and always shared their parcels with others. With the children I remained an outsider for a long time. Their community was already established. Feelings of liking that sparkled in children disappeared just as swiftly, sometimes for no reason at all. It could be simply because one's mood had changed or because one felt like being capricious. Perhaps one just wanted to feel unhappy or unjustly injured. You only needed to attack whoever was at hand, to provoke a quarrel.

Basically all children are greedy. Even though these children had so little, they were no different. They treasured their little property: toys, treats, drawing pencils, paper. They only agreed to share them with other children who had nothing after long entreaties from the teachers who were upset by such selfishness. With a child who also possessed something, however, they tried to negotiate some business relationship based on the principle "You give me something, I'll give you something."

The grown-ups worried about their relatives, felt sympathy for one another, and did their best to help the ones that were extremely unwell. The children as a rule thought only of themselves and vigilantly guarded their own private interests.

But children grow and therefore change. They can learn to love, to share, to care for others. The process went slowly with us, however, while the fight for leadership, authority, and superiority in any petty matter was violent and took strength, time, and nerve. Three years of concurrent growth like that sometimes seemed like a lingering disease.

The climate for relationships was unhealthy. I exploded on many occasions. I would react to any assault, even an imaginary assault on my person, by becoming aggressive, irritable, and cruel. I thirsted for revenge. I nursed plans of the best ways to punish, to hurt the "enemy." First there were wounds on my self-esteem or encounters with treachery and gossip. When I finally noticed that I too had become a gossip, a traitor, or a miser, then would come feelings of shame and suffering. But to admit such sins was beyond capability. Being tortured by these nasty deeds, whether one's own or someone else's, was like suffering from a complicated case of scarlet fever.

Seven

In the winter, our teacher read Chekhov's *Kashtanka* to us. During my "bed life," reading was as important as meeting people from the outside world. It was as if I was experiencing the events in the books.

It seemed to be broad daylight and sunshine whenever we listened to *Kashtanka*. There was life all around. Still, the story of the death of the goose, Ivan Ivanovitch, filled me with horror. Then I felt I was listening to it in the darkness, all alone. The story is so simple! Nothing out of the ordinary: a room, a candle, a cat, a dog, a goose, and a man: all of them restless. The goose, for some reason, is not asleep, but sitting on the floor with its wings spread and its bill open. The man sees that the goose is dying and there is nothing that can be done. He takes the candle and leaves the room. The man carries away the candle with its little light jumping on the dirty wallpaper and ceiling, and it seems to the dog that there's a stranger standing in the room, invisible and shapeless and impossible to bite. It's death. Both the cat and the dog are sick at heart. Death sometimes looks at them through the dark window, sometimes stands very close, so close that they can feel its presence but have nothing to drive it away.

It was death's simple ordinariness in the story that frightened me most of all. I was used to thinking that sudden death only came when one had committed a grave sin deserving death, as in Gogol's *Horrible Revenge.* As for the normal person, death would have to inform him beforehand of its coming, so that he could prepare himself. The signs of an approaching death were mysterious omens, such as seeing the dead in your sleep or contracting a lingering disease. If the person had committed no evil deeds, though, death wouldn't be too frightening for him. He'd only have that unpleasant feeling one has before an operation or a painful wound dressing, for he'd know he's passing into a different life.

There was no anticipation of another life in Chekhov's *Kashtanka.* The death was not a passing on, but a horrifying annihilation. There was only a terrifying cold corpse left, with outstretched limbs and grimace.

This view of the world was repulsively convincing in its simplicity. Death might come in the night, right into the room where I was lying?! Now I was afraid to sleep with my face uncovered. I hid under the blanket and pulled it over my head so that death wouldn't notice me, wouldn't recognize me, wouldn't look into my closed eyes, and would pass me by. I tried to breathe very quietly so as not to attract its attention.

In the dark, when the lights went out, the worst memories of my life haunted me. ...

Papa had brought me to the forest-steppe experimental station, where I spent the summer as usual with Granny's brother Nikolai Kuzmitch. Too soon, Papa was taking me away again, because the war had suddenly started. He was wearing a white shirt but no jacket. It was hot. He held the reins like a true coachman, anxiously spurring on the horse. He kept looking around in a worried fashion. He turned his young, spectacled face toward me, looked at me inquiringly, and frowned with pity. He knew that every jerk of the wagon over a bump hurt me. In those days, they thought I had simply bruised my back. They didn't suspect it was tuberculosis.

We were riding along an endless, narrow lane. Bushes with bright red leaves stood along each side. We were riding, but it seemed we didn't move forward, only stayed in one place. The wagon wheels squeaked, the horse stamped the ground. But it was in vain. The same red bushes on both sides of the road were rooted to the spot, suffocated in the dust and heat. There had been no rain for a long time, and the air was choked with dust. It looked like a fog, but it carried no water. A dense, caustic haze had enveloped the world. Narrow leaves were ablaze above, while I was on fire with pain below. My back ached. Every bump evoked stinging pain and misery. Papa's white shirt blinded me like the February snow.

Then there was the gray city, and then the gray dust and black curtains over the window. We went to a dusty room where, in my imagination, things turned crazy all of a sudden and escaped from their corners, crawled out of the wardrobe, and lay in dead heaps. Papa packed my things for evacuation. Who should I go with? Where to? I had no idea. Grown-ups had plans of their own. I wondered at the strips of yellowish newspaper, with faded letters, on the window. The windows in the house across the street also carried long Xs of faded yellow. This was to protect from broken glass in case of bombing. We lived so close to the Kremlin, we were under heavy bombardment.

On top of it all—a gas mask! Papa brought home a gas mask and put it on suddenly. A rubber head with dim glasses of eyes goggled at me, with a hanging corrugated trunk-nose. This dead rubber creature dressed in Papa's suit waved the rubber trunk and held out Papa's hands to me!

I screamed so loudly that even my own ears plugged up. *They've replaced Papa with this thing!*

He pulled the gas mask off and laughed. He kept saying, "It's me! Me! Look at me!" But I feared him all day long after that. What if he turned into *that* again, with no human face! The gas mask, lying on a chair, was only pretending to be a harmless thing. It could come to life and stick to someone's face whenever it liked. Papa took the gas mask out to the corridor.

Another frightening memory of that time was about coats. Next to our door there hung black coats with long sleeves. It seemed to me that in the sleeves' invisible arms were hiding. They always tried to grab me when I ran past them. I would run with a yell to Papa or to my nanny in the kitchen when they lingered there too long and I was unable to wait anymore.

In the hospital, not only memories, but nightmares tortured me. Here's my recollection of one such nightmare:

> *I follow the evacuated women and crawl under a train car in order to get across the tracks. On the other side of the rails is our car with our belongings and a warm stove. Suddenly the train above my head gives a jerk, the wheels roll noiselessly, and something clangs. One more second and I'll be cut to pieces! Sharp coal dust flies into my face. I have a loaf of bread in my bosom. I say to myself, 'Pity, now it will be wasted!'*

I yelled in my sleep from nightmares every night. I woke everyone. Then I was taken to an isolation ward and treated with bromine and rest.

When nightmares ceased, I had dreams like this one:

> *I am running across a vast meadow to Aunt Elena's house. The lighted windows are open and I hear a piano tinkling inside. It is already dark. I run over the dark grass. My feet grow lighter and lighter and then I take off and fly, not even touching the ground. I fly over the grass and I can, at will, dip my feet into it, like into cool night water. I am overwhelmed with joy. It fills me like a pre-war helium balloon. I rise over the roof of the house where music is splashing and the summer sky is blue with light cotton-wool clouds. Am I so happy that I can't help flying? Or is it the flight that makes me happy? ...*

Then the door of the isolation ward rattled. The wheels of the medicine cart rumbled on the floor. Something gave a chink, or a nasty medical sound, heralding an injection or some other misfortune. Hard hands of a stranger stuck an ice cold thermometer into my armpit. I opened my eyes and saw the hospital window, still full of impenetrable darkness, and the white ceiling with a naked, glaring lamp. I was back on the ground, bound firmly and in winter.

In contrast to my summer dream, the winter rudely intruded itself with its long, dark mornings and sharp attacks of cold. Cold came from many sources: from the thermometer, from the water in the wash basin, from the window pane thrown open, even from the over-starched towel stiff as card-board.

EIGHT

Despite everything, I was fine in the isolation room. I discovered one day that I could read and now I always had a source of joy—tattered pages and rare faded pictures. I discovered this ability to read quite unexpectedly in the ward, when my neighbor let me look at the pictures in her brand new ABC book. I studied them closely. There was a boy walking somewhere with a flag in his outstretched hands, a girl playing with a cat, and a mother pouring water from a jug onto a baby's cupped palms. I stared at the letters, and recognition began to dawn. I found myself reading the words!

Papa had started to teach me the alphabet when I was about four. I had to stand in front of the chair, on which he spelled out words with letters: p-a-p-a, n-a-n-n-y. How extremely boring it was! I received something tasty as a reward if I managed to recognize a letter. At the time, it seemed the only effect of this simple method of training was to teach me to hate any kind of learning.

Then there was the war, evacuation, and illness. Much of what had happened in our pre-war life gradually faded from my memory. Only occasionally, obscure episodes emerged like long-forgotten dreams.

Three years later, though, those lessons from the pre-war life that now seemed only a dream were proved to not have been in vain. I could read all that was in the ABC book. Hurray! My bed neighbor, the owner of the book, at first didn't believe I was actually reading. She received the book as a present for her seventh birthday, because she was to start school in the fall. I didn't have long to wait before turning seven—only a fall, winter, and spring. I too was promised an ABC book for my birthday.

"You're not reading. You're just guessing what's written there from the pictures!" my neighbor said. "Any fool can do that. How about trying to read a book *without* pictures?" She threw onto my bed a wornout book with the cover ripped off. The words in it were not in lines, but in columns.

To my own surprise, I slowly but loudly read:

В синем море волны плещут
В синем небе звезды блещут

In the blue sea the waves play,
In the blue sky the stars shine.

It was so wonderful, that my voice faltered. I paused until my excitement calmed down, and then I started to read it all. I decided that one had to read aloud, and not only out loud but *loud*. It didn't occur to me that I could read to myself. My voice rang with excitement. I was nearly shouting and very soon everyone was tired of me. But I couldn't stop, couldn't part from this magic book. I even loved its smell, the smell of dusty paper, with its letters and words that were so nice to sing, to shout, that charmed me so much. They tried to take the book away from me, but I screeched and bawled. I hid the book under my blanket and would sooner have parted with life than to have parted with it. Then I was separated into an isolation room together with my precious book and left alone.

I could savor it as much as I liked. I shouted aloud all of Pushkin's fairy tales printed in this book several times over till

I was quite hoarse. I enjoyed immensely the very process of reading. I read with increasing fluency. I memorized verses by heart. It was as if I was sledding down from the top of a high mountain. I believed more and more in my own abilities. The music of the verse captured my imagination and emotions and carried me away upwards to the huge night sky where stars were shining. I was so sorry for the unjustly hurt princess in one of Pushkin's tales. She was tricked by her jealous sisters and torn from her husband. She and her newborn son were trapped in a barrel and thrown into the ocean to be tossed about and lost in the great wide sea. What a joy when the story had a happy ending.

My life was dramatically changed. The powerlessness and helplessness of a person who had literally been tied to the bed for two years, was now defeated. I fell under the power of a new, mighty, and mysterious lord, the written word, and it filled me with pride. How boring it is to belong only to yourself, to your needs and desires. How wonderful it is to belong to something that is higher than yourself—to the written word, to spirit, stars, ideas! I was denied the joy of the world outside with its impressions, movements, and changes of forms, colors, and smells. But I found a different source of happiness: the music of verse.

The charm of words became real to me. I made one discovery after another. It was as if I tasted the words. I held them in my mouth, yielding to the play of my imagination. Take the word *thunder*. *Thun-* is something coming closer and closer from far away, and already threatening. It then stretches, rolls into a long booming *-derrrr*. Then it suddenly stops with a sigh, a sigh made with full lungs, a sigh combined with the hum of rain on the iron roof of a house in my forest steppe. And *drop*, what a charming word! First, *d-* ... a wet shining dot is born at the end of a tree branch behind the window. Then it grows and expands: *ro-* ... and at last falls down sparkling: *-p. ... Drop!*

I lay there alone, reading everything that was given to me. I looked out the window at the tree limb, at the clouds melting in the blue sky, at a bird that dared to walk along the cornice. There was no one in the world happier or richer than I. For now I saw clouds and branches and faces differently. Everything turned out to be full of mystery. All things can be named, and this brought to life a new essence in people, events, even objects. I saw a nurse's face approaching me with thick black brows and a big mole on her cheek. A little tuft of hair was growing on the mole. One could see the pores on her nose, and the whites of her eyes were covered with thin red veins. But her eyes were alive and moist. There was something shining in them. They looked at me as if from some other world. They looked worried, questioning.

To myself I whispered, "Nurse." The collar of her dress was sticking out from under the white uniform. That dress represented life outside the hospital. It was something from another world, a place I couldn't go. I was intensely curious to get acquainted with it. But the nurse let me step into her world only for a couple of seconds. I didn't have enough time to examine anything properly. I got just a moment's glance in her eyes to see this other world, and then the door banged shut in my face. Her eyes silenced the question. They had an estranged, aloof look. When she returned, the collar of the white coat was buttoned and the nurse was holding out to me a plate of porridge. Her face was as far from me as the moon hidden by the clouds. I was saddened by the transformation.

The music of verse, on the contrary, generously opened itself and gave itself to me. I sang poems. I talked aloud to myself, and the words tickled my throat. I fell asleep and woke up with verses on my lips. In my dreams I sang them and composed others myself. It was such a pity I couldn't remember them when I woke up. All that was left was a mixture of happiness and sadness.

NINE

I'm not saying that I hadn't known poetry. In the hospital we learned many verses and songs, such as: *Ten-ten-poteten, the Fence is Higher Than the Town; Everything's Still Till the Dawn;* and *The International.*

Poems and songs of miserable children seemed especially touching. Once I recited this poem:

The eyes of a seven-year-old girl
Are like two faded little lights.
There are signs of great and heavy misery
On her little face.
She never replies to whatever you ask her;
If you make a joke—you get silence in reply,
As if she's not seven, not eight,
But many bitter years old.
All of a sudden, as if a fresh wind
Has passed over the child's face,
Winged by hope,
She dashes to a soldier.
Looking at him with her clear eyes,
She seeks protection:
'They were breaking mama's arms,
Kill them all, till there are none left.'

I wanted to grab a rifle and dash into the thick of the battle! I imagined a hefty German soldier breaking the arms of a little woman while a frightened child cried and screamed in the background. I gritted my teeth with hatred.

Our hatred fed on poems, songs, and stories about suffering children and heroic adults that made us boil with righteous wrath. We all wanted to be heroes. A striving for martyrdom was instilled in us. We absorbed the idea that to be a hero was the best thing possible. We all believed ourselves capable of performing some daring exploit.

Oh, if someone had only told me then that I had German blood in my veins!—that my grandfather was a German. What would I have done? Very likely no one would have befriended me. I would have been taunted and beaten. Perhaps, in my mind, I would've divided Germans into the good and the bad, and I would've believed myself one of the good. But in any case my hatred would have been lessened. I would've understood that not all Germans were fiends. Very likely I would've tried to conceal my secret. This is what I did later at school. I tried to conceal the fact that my Papa was a Jew, though my last name—Mashbitz—announced it loudly.

Oh, this perfidious desire to be no worse than others! The voice of conscience becomes barely audible, barely discernible. How can one protect that which everyone hates?

Later, Granny Zhenia told me about pogroms during her childhood. She was four or five. Her family lived in the center of Saratov on the second floor of a spacious, roomy house. The ground floor was occupied by her father's shop. The family were Russian Orthodox of a group called Old Believers.

On pogrom days, Granny's mother pulled down the blinds. In the dark morning hours, her nanny led a group of dark-eyed children, women, and old men in skullcaps and side curls through back lanes, through the inner yard and into the back entrance of Great-Grandfather's shop. They hid in the wide anteroom and on the staircase, pressing close to each other, sitting in silence on bundles of clothing and blankets. The frightened children didn't cry; the old men didn't cough; and the women didn't chat or whisper.

Granny Zhenia and her brothers pulled aside the edge of the heavy curtain a little and peeped down at the street. There streamed an agitated crowd. Dirty splashes of drunken swear words were tossed into the air. Clubs and iron rods were brandished. A hot wind raced down the street and flung dust into the windowpane. There was the sound of heavy crude boots and the glimpse of dark spots of sweat on chintz backs. Granny Zhenia told me that she started to shiver all over from fear and dashed away from the window. She hid under a table and pulled down the corner of the velvet tablecloth.

Nanny stood by the window repeating, "Ah, here's a joy for the devil! Demons in hell must be jumping with joy!" Granny's brother, thirteen-year-old Grisha, who attended the gymnasium and was an honors pupil, grumbled, showing off with his newly-acquired atheism before Nanny. "How do you know what is joy for devils? There aren't any devils at all! It's all imagination!"

"Ah, if only they didn't exist. Who then eggs these stupid thugs on?" Nanny grieved. "Who spurs *any* evil deed? Ah, it is so hot, the wind is, it burned my face as I walked outside. It is as if it is not from the steppe, as if from hell this wind is. Devils thirst for blood." The little girl shaking under the table, my future Granny Zhenia, believed Nanny, not Grisha, much as she wanted to think there were no such things as demons. But who then drives insanity into these big, strong men, screaming below?

Years later, my mother would bring home her future husband: a dark-eyed, merry Jew.

He introduced her to his family, also. The Mashbitz family table in the Pechatnikov lane apartment was laid for forty persons. At the table there gathered a lot of young, energetic people. There were doctors, engineers, biologists, and literati. Parents, six sisters and three brothers with their families, and relatives from other places all talked, gesticulated, laughed, feasted and cast occasional glances at the fair-haired sister-in-law with a porcelain-like blush on her cheeks. My two cousins, little girls then, who were present at that party, would tell me that my mother seemed to them a beauty most fair, delicate, and unearthly.

In 1933 my father's elder brother would surrender his room to the newlyweds, my parents. In the '40s my mother's mother, at the risk of detainment, would provide food for a prisoner, that very brother. He had been a philologist, a former respected "red professor," but now in the prison camp he was a bootmaker. Father's sisters would save me from death in 1942. Knots of destiny were being tied at the table laid for forty persons, at which were seated people of Jewish, Russian, and German heritage.

In my youth I found something delightful lying on Granny Zhenia's table: two heavy lenses with pictures of Germany glued to the reverse side, a keepsake of her life there. One of the pictures depicted a rural landscape, the other an urban scene. Trees and houses seemed lifelike in the depth of the thick glass. Setting the lens at a different angle, I could arrange a sunrise over the city or the field: the sun rolled up from over the forested mountains; the hillsides warmed up; the trees rejoiced. I'd light up patches of sunset color in the windows of neat houses with turrets and red peaked roofs. I examined a wonderful strange country in those lenses and I dreamed of becoming a tiny fly and flying to these little white houses. Perhaps kind people lived there, like Karl Ivanovitch from Tolstoy's *Childhood.*

And there were Granny's books from Germany, with their Gothic font, thin paper and etchings, and fascinating illustrations of castles, gardens, and ladies in long robes.

A thick envelope contained photos that I would spend hours examining. There was Mama, seven years old, long-legged and tall, standing in the middle of a motley group of kids ranging in age from four to ten. All were skinny and poorly dressed. Those were the neighborhood children she befriended in Berlin. She learned German quickly and spoke it correctly. She carried her friends away with play acting; that group in this blurred and faded photograph was, in fact, a troupe company. I don't know whether they performed for an audience or simply dressed up for their own pleasure and performed something in the apartment that Granny Zhenia rented.

Germany suffered from terrible inflation. People lived in hunger. Granny Zhenia found a job in the Soviet trade commission. She got her salary in dollars and could feed her daughter's friends. It was a real treat for these children in decrepit clothes with stretched hems and mended pants to wrap up in a white tulle pillow cover and imagine themselves princesses or to put an aluminum saucepan on their heads, take a stick sword or a long-handled letter opener and turn into knights, protectors of fair ladies. In this old photograph, knights and princesses surrounded the long-legged girl, my future mama, a German-Russian.

Can it be true that fifteen years later these little knights with emaciated faces put on real helmets and black uniforms with a skull on the sleeve? Did they turn into mere cannon fodder, driven to conquer my country?

Primitive nationalism was not the only thing that found fertile soil in us children. Class hatred and proletariat arrogance sprouted and thrived. After I left the sanatorium I lived with Granny Zhenia. When I was in fourth grade, a classmate named Verka, who was the daughter of a fire brigade driver, came to visit me. I showed her our family album.

"And this here is my grandfather. You see, here he and Granny are selling chamomiles. These are paper flowers, made by students and sold to raise money for treatment of poor students who had consumption. You see, Granny is wearing a ribbon over her shoulder. On it is written, 'Fight against consumption.'"

"Why does your grandfather have shoulder straps? And here he's wearing a white tunic! Mighty rich from his looks! What, is he a white officer? Where does he live now?" Verka looked at me with suspicion.

How close the enemy turns out to be entrenched! Scared, I exclaimed, "He died long ago! Mama was still a child. And he wasn't an officer at all. He was a student railroader. They have uniforms with shoulder straps. You remember Petka, who came from the railway technical school from Ukhta? Our boys looked at his black overcoat with gold buttons and wanted to be railway students."

"Oh, I se-e-e. ..." Verka screwed up her eyes with significance. She must have been disappointed that she hadn't found out a guilty family secret and unmasked me. Even though she came for a visit, she hated me for some reason. I sensed it and tried to defeat her hatred.

"I know ...," Verka accused after some consideration, "students and secondary schoolboys were all from wealthy families. There, look at the faces of those relatives of yours, how clean they are. And their clothes—all lace and brand-new uniforms ... surely not from the common people."

"Grandfather's dad, an engineer, died when he was five. His mother raised him alone. She didn't get married a second time. She may be wearing lace and gloves, but that is because she worked at a confectioner's shop. It was simply a matter of fashion. Fashion was all lacy then."

"She worked? You expect me to believe you? In such a coat, with a parasol, she worked? No, she's a fine lady, that's clear as day! Shop assistants are never like that. Look at my aunt Raya. Does she walk with a parasol and patent leather shoes? It's dirty in the shop. It stinks of herring and is mighty cold because the door is wide open all winter. The shop assistant wears a quilted jacket and an oilcloth apron. Her hands are greasy from the herring. Your Granny likely had manicured nails. A fine lady she was, and a maid did the washing for her. Not even a broom would one hold with such fine fingers. All your relations are wealthy people!"

"You are wrong," I cried defensively. "Granny and her brothers are in nice uniforms because they were all students. They were orphans as well. They lived very poorly. They studied and worked. There were seven children with an illiterate mother, left without a father. But they were all such excellent students that they were allowed to go to school free. They tutored rich pupils who struggled with their homework. Granny went to work when she was ten!"

But Verka sniffed distrustfully and tossed the album aside. With my lies I had betrayed all my kin out of fear. I would've preferred that instead of all these clever, handsome, cultured faces in my family album there had stared out coarse faces with traces of hard drinking and ignorance. I never showed our family photos to any of my classmates again.

Besides nationalism and class hatred, our lives were poisoned by spy mania that infected me in the long run as well. My source of contagion was a book about a grandfather spy who hid his portable wireless in the cellar and concealed the wire in a table leg. Everyone thought this grandfather a good man who dearly loved his orphan granddaughter, the best pupil in school. Then one day this girl hanged herself! The grandfather barely survived his grief, and everybody pitied him. But it all turned out to be bogus. A clever detective proved that the grandfather had hanged the child himself. The granddaughter went to the cellar to get some potatoes just as her grandfather was communicating over the wireless with the fascists. He grabbed the girl and hanged her so she couldn't tell anyone he was a spy for the enemy.

This book scared me to no end. My own granny had been convicted on suspicion of espionage! Granny laughed and said that her "case" was "in name only" and that many people suffered from cases "in name only." But I undertook a search of the whole house. The only suspicious things I found were two gold teeth wrapped in paper lying under the socks in a wardrobe drawer.

There were no wires in the chair or table legs. That set my mind at rest a bit. Neither were there any masked wires stretching from the cellar trap door into the kitchen. The trap door was built from exactly the same boards as the rest of the kitchen floor. I'd been inside the cellar with Granny and seen only potatoes, bottles of berry preserves on dusty shelves, sour cabbage and pickled mushrooms in cans. Granny kept no secrets in the cellar.

One thing still bothered me. Whose were the teeth, and why were they hidden under the socks? I ransacked all the corners. In the desk I found a bundle of letters. They dealt only with me, with how I crawled, what I could say, how I pulled the cat's tail, nothing spy-like. But still, why were those gold teeth wrapped in a scrap of paper? There had to be something behind it. As it turned out, those were Granny's gold crowns. She had asked the doctor to take them off and replace them with iron ones so that no fool would get the idea to kill her for the gold.

Prejudice abounded. In Siberia during the evacuation, the kids there gave offensive nicknames to us evacuated Muscovites and showed openly their disdain. "You Muscovites! You have started this war!" Some snot-nosed primitive would brandish his fist in my face and say, "I'd put you with your face to the wall and machine-gun you: *tach-tach-tak-tak-tak*!"

I have other memories of how I was treated in Siberia. I remember scrubbing the endless floor in the big cabin and moaning from the pain in my back. Tuberculosis smoldered in my bones. I remember a fussy baby, huge and heavy. I watched over him and carried him in my arms. He didn't want to walk himself and screamed deafeningly whenever I made an attempt to set him on the floor to give a rest to my constantly aching back.

I remember how water would splash from a pail over my feet as I struggled to carry it to the kitchen garden. The vegetable beds stretched to the horizon. Pail after pail, pail after pail I carried water to the garden. Quietly and with desperation I cried that the pails were unbearably heavy. Later, I had to hoe the potatoes. After several thrusts of the chopper into the soil I could barely lift it again, and the backache got fiercer. But there would be no rest and no complaints to anyone, or

I would be beaten.

The landlady's son was a hunchbacked boy. He felt offended by life and vented on me. Once he knocked me down when I was sent to get a new broom. I fell with my back to the floor. He laughed down at me, "A hunchback you'll be, like me! A hunchbacked Muscovite!"

The pain was so great I couldn't even take a breath, to say nothing of crying out. The floor seemed to rush towards me as I fell. I writhed for a long time before I could regain my breath. Later, in the hospital, they tried to wean me from the habit of drawing my head into my shoulders like a turtle and covering myself with crossed arms, ready to deflect the blow. I did this whenever someone came up to me to pat my head or to give me something. Stray dogs jump away like that when someone holds out a hand toward them suddenly.

Here is one more hard, nightmare-like reminiscence of my hunchbacked master. ... I had a caterpillar named Katya that lived in a matchbox. I felt remorseful that I was keeping a live being captive, but the desire to see the magical metamorphosis of a caterpillar into a butterfly was too great. I took care of it. I checked whether it was getting enough air, whether it had enough light and space. I made bedding for it from soft leaves. I left a small chink for the air—a small window it couldn't squeeze through but could breathe through. I kept the matchbox in my pocket and every few minutes put my hand inside to feel the box. I took it out and held it to my ear, listening to the mysterious rustle inside. I plucked the juiciest blades of grass and leaves and pushed them into the matchbox, so that the caterpillar ate, got fatter, and came closer and closer to becoming a butterfly. Sometimes I tried to guess from the rustling inside whether it was still a caterpillar or by now a butterfly. I dreamed of the moment when I would open the matchbox and would not see the cousin of the nasty worm. Instead, crawling on fading leaves, a butterfly with large wings would flit out. It would flutter off, and I would run after it on the grass.

"What's that you have there?" my hunchbacked master asked, having noticed me holding something in my hand.

"A caterpillar in a box. It'll soon turn into a butterfly."

"Give it here!" He twisted my hand until my fingers opened and the matchbox dropped to his feet. My torturer called two boys who giggled to see me weep as they executed the caterpillar on a large stone. I stood frozen like a pillar, wracked with misery, hatred, and helplessness.

In the hospital in Moscow, the girls and I also tried to make a butterfly from a caterpillar, but failed. One day we found the matchbox empty. The caterpillar had managed to escape and got lost on the cracked floor of the veranda.

Another change came into my life because of prejudice. I had turned sixteen and it was time for me to get my identification papers. Granny Zhenia, who had suffered a lot because of her German name, Herbst, called for a consultation with my dad's sisters. They had also endured a lot of adversities because of their Jewish name, Mashbitz. They decided that I had to take Granny Zhenia's Russian maiden name, Vekhova. Otherwise, good-bye higher education! Being gifted would not help a bit.

Convincingly, they recalled numerous sad stories of talented children they knew who had the disadvantage of bearing a name that sounded unusual to the Russian ear. And so I became Marianna Vekhova.

TEN

In every community you need a leader, whether it is a community of animals, birds, or children. We hospital patients experienced a lengthy era of leadership by a cunning "walking" girl named Taika. At ten years of age she was a master at stirring up a squabble and then disappearing at the hottest moment. At the precise time that a teacher would burst in with a searching look and accusation on the lips, Taika was nowhere to be seen. The penalty, as always, awaited not Taika, but another victim of hers.

Taika triumphed and was glad for her artfulness. She kept bothering us with her sexual fantasies. She arranged dancing at night and pillow fights. She egged on the "lying" girls to get out of their plaster cots, a thing that was punished severely, because one could easily ruin the results of a long and laborious treatment. I never took part in the wild nightlife only because I slept so soundly that nothing could rouse me from slumber. While I slept, secrets were told in whispers. Dances were performed on tiptoes. And pillows flew about noiselessly like big-bellied spirits. In the morning all the pillow down, all the scraps of paper, and the lost towels were always found under my bed. The evidence convicted me, and my ignorance looked like obstinacy and artfulness. Therefore the punishment followed immediately.

Taika rejoiced. The ward kept silent. In her control over us, Taika reigned. She didn't tolerate friendships between the girls, and always tried to break them, to spoil them. She set girls against each other. She kindled quarrels. She plotted clever intrigues. Even five years after I'd left the hospital I still recalled Taika with horror. She haunted me in my dreams and I was afraid I'd wake up and see her in our house with that nasty grin of hers. Her sly grin seemed to say that she knew something shameful and hidden about me, something that would make people draw away from me should they learn of it. I hated that grin of hers.

Taika's thin little face had prominent cheek bones and sharp eyes as dark as coal. Her shiny black hair had something serpent-like about it. Very rarely in my life have I chanced to meet a person with such a strong, destructive temperament. Taika was probably annoyed at our clumsy simple-heartedness, our childish stupidity. Her life before the hospital must have been full of experiences that were quite unknown to us. She clearly had matured early, and we weren't any kind of company for her. Children like her, too mature for their age because of their experience or early development, need an equal friend-rival. And they need an authority. In any other environment our Taika wouldn't be able to go on trying her hand in intrigues and exerting her power over the rest of us.

Taika was my vicious and powerful enemy. I don't know why I irritated her more than anyone else did, but so it was. We lay bound to our plaster cots, while Taika stumped adroitly with her crutches in the corridor. She could freely leave the ward and when she entered it again it was with a mysterious and important look. The gleam in her eye seemed to say that she'd learned something extraordinary out there in the world that we were denied.

Oh, how much we all wanted to have a chance to be out in the corridor! It was from that corridor that our relatives appeared from liberty when they came to visit us. Sometimes rain drops or melting snowflakes glittered in the nurse's hair when she entered the ward having swiftly dashed into the entrance door through the corridor. She was still fanned with wind, merry and flushed from hurrying, with her cheeks fresh. Every time the door opened, the ones whose beds were close could glimpse a red carpet and the long shadowy reaches of the corridor.

Although our world was very constricted we had plenty of occupations. At the music lessons we sang songs and learned to play the kinds of instruments one could play lying in bed: tambourine, triangles, cymbals, and harmonica. We were taught to sew little bags, to hem and make lacy edges to handkerchiefs, to work with a crochet hook, to weave rugs and baskets, and to make artificial flowers. These were all skills that could be useful later in life. A lot of us were destined to remain cripples, and what kind of life would it be without some interesting occupation?

One day the teacher told us that soon we'd be celebrating Victory, because the war was to end very soon. Our troops were marching over Germany. It was time we started preparing for the great holiday! Gladly we learned poems and songs suitable for the occasion.

The best item on our program was a song about poppies. We were to sing it and to accompany it on our tambourines, triangles, and harmonicas. As we finished our part, the teacher repeated the tune on the piano alone. At that moment we were to lift up our hands with paper poppies that we would make ourselves, and the "walking" Taika would go around all the beds and collect the flowers. She'd take the bunch of paper flowers to the portrait of Comrade Stalin, decorated with scarlet ribbons.

It took us some two weeks to manufacture the poppies. After a lot of practice, they started to turn out well. One had to cut out the petals from red crepe paper, and the leaves from the green paper. We carefully smoothed every petal so that it became rounded like a spoon. We twisted light green tissue paper around the end of the stem, and tied it half an inch lower with a thread. That was the pistil of the poppy. Then we glued short black threads all around the pistil and got the stamen. After that we glued the petals one after the other. The pistil with the black stamen must not stick too far out of the flower, though one was not to hide it too deeply in the flower either. To guess how far it was going to stick out when you glued on the first petal was by no means an easy thing to do. How many times we had to do it over and over again!

At last we fixed the blossom with a narrow green bond of tissue paper, wrapping the stem and adding leaves. The work required a lot of attention and patience. If you tried to work too fast it all went wrong and crooked, not at all like the wonderful sample poppy made by the teacher. And a bad flower cannot be given to Comrade Stalin!

Fingers became sticky with glue, and everything stuck to them. Something or other constantly got lost on the blanket: either the rod stem or a petal. Nevertheless we made lots of poppies! We had a rehearsal and were delighted: so beautifully we had done it. And so Victory Day came.

The radio gave us triumphant speeches all day long, plus it broadcast marches and merry songs. A genuine combat commander promised to come to our celebration! He had been wounded in a battle, and now had finished a course of treatment. He had plenty of medals! We anxiously awaited him.

We longed to see a commander in flesh and blood. Not in a movie, but right here, in our corridor. Besides, a lot of us dreamed of asking him, "Have you perhaps run into my papa at the front? His name is ..."

At last we were rolled out into the corridor. All the wards were there, from the little ones to the secondary-school children. The beds were lined up along the wall. Each ward performed some items for the large concert. Then there was the commander; smiling as he walked along the aisle. He was not very old and he limped a little. He came to a halt at the end of the corridor where the palm tree spread its leaves under a large portrait of Stalin. Next to the commander stood our doctor, Vagram Petrovitch, and all the doctors, nurses and aides. The teachers hovered round our beds in anxiety.

Of course, I don't remember much of the items of that concert. I only remember how we worried, waiting for our turn. We were hiding the poppies under the sheets, and we were so much afraid of rumpling them. The song about the poppies was to be the last one in the concert. The teacher worried that Taika might confuse things. She had to bring the bunch of flowers first up to the portrait of Comrade Stalin and then hand them to the commander, because he had been protecting us from Germans.

At last the long-awaited moment came. Tambourines, triangles, and mouth organs started to play, and we sang:

Look at the poppies, look at the poppies!
Red and beautiful, they bloom in the field!

We slowly raised the flowers in our hands, and it was merrier and merrier in the corridor, and redder and redder with poppies, and our voices got stronger:

The wind comes, the wind comes
It bends to earth, the thin stems ...

We waved the poppies, and it looked like a field of flowers rippled by the wind. We continued, inspired:

Little Maika went out onto a lawn ...

Thumping with her crutches, Taika appeared from behind the beds. She started to collect the flowers, and as she walked around all the beds, we kept repeating like a gramophone record stuck in one grove:

Little Maika went out onto a lawn,
Little Maika went out onto a lawn ...

Taika toddled to the last bed in the row and "plucked" the last flower. The huge bouquet hid her face completely, and she could barely hold it in her hand. Now she had to walk leaning only on one crutch. But the flowers swayed very beautifully from her uneven tread. We struck the tambourines and triangles with our hands, free by now, in triumph, and burst out:

For our dear Stalin
She plucked a flower bouquet.

Taika's second crutch, which she had left leaning against someone's bed, slid on the slippery floor and dropped with a crash. Taika didn't even look back and walked up to the portrait of Stalin, leaning on the remaining crutch and pressing the wire stems of our poppies closer to her bosom. She let the nearest nurse hold her crutch, and, swaying a bit, held out the bunch to the portrait with both her hands. Then we repeated in unison:

For our dear Stalin
She plucked a flower bouquet.

Taika now stood firmly, and we roared in chorus:

Thanks to the great Stalin for our happy childhood!

Taika shoved the bouquet at the commander, right into his face. She was tired from standing on one leg only without having a crutch to lean on. The commander took the bunch of paper poppies and he burst into tears. He buried his face into the flowers. The little tousled Taika stood in front of him with her face raised to him and her mouth opened. Her gray gown always went awry as she walked with her crutches, and it gathered into a bunch on her chest and her back, as if she had hunches there. Taika wasn't hunchbacked. She had a problem in her hip joint and her right leg was much shorter because of it. So she limped—no big deal! The commander must have thought she was lame and hunchbacked and felt pity for her.

We were simply shocked to see a real combat commander start crying all of a sudden, and on top of everything, in the middle of a celebration, in front of the whole blessed world and Comrade Stalin's portrait! How could that be? He was grown up! He was a military man! He was a commander! We lay as quiet as mice.

But then Doctor Vagram Petrovitch smiled at Taika, put an arm around her shoulders, kissed her cheek and started to applaud. All our nurses, doctors, teachers and older children started to applaud also. Then we joined in. Taika, flushed and proud, returned to her dropped crutch.

"But my Dad never cries!" we said to each other later, when we had been rolled back to our ward.

Our song with poppies turned out to be the best one! We got more applause than anyone else! We received a lot of praises for the poppies.

Yes, our poppies looked just like real flowers. But the sun never warmed them, wind never moved them, bees never got into them, and morning dew never fell on them. One could not sprinkle them with the water of life, or they would get soggy and the paper would fall apart. The bare wire would stick out and threads smeared with glue pellets would hang down helplessly.

But they will stand nicely next to Comrade Stalin's portrait on the shelf! Anyone who will look at them will say what good girls we are, with such talented hands. Maybe someone will even tell Comrade Stalin about our poppies. And he will be very glad. ...

Life followed its normal course. My spine got stronger and I was allowed to get up. First I was put upright onto the floor next to the bed for two minutes at a time. I felt so giddy. But my time was over before I barely had time to feel something. Slowly I was able to stand longer, first for four minutes, then for six, and so on till I stood for ten minutes. Then it all started again: two, four, six. From the early morning I started preparing for the great moment of getting up! I was not dizzy anymore; only my weak legs shook. It turns out that one sees everything in a totally different way when standing. The entire world looks different. What bliss—to be able to stand!

Then I was allowed to stand for twenty minutes. A nurse came; she untied the straps and took off the bagels from my arms and legs. I unlaced myself fast as lightning and caught envious looks cast at me from neighboring beds. I was inserted into a thick plaster corset and laced tightly. At last I stood on a rag rug that I wove myself for that purpose. I stood holding onto the cold iron bedrails, and examined the well-known ward with new eyes. The walls drew closer upon me, the ward became smaller and more accessible. Dreams could come true! *Just wait till I learn to walk. I'll walk to the piano and touch the keys, and if someone drops a toy, I'll pick it up!*

I learned to get around my bed, holding first at the back and then at the iron frame, by moving my feet inch by inch. At last the great day came when a nurse led me out into the mysterious, endlessly-long corridor. Active life bustled there. Footsteps echoed, as people carried our food, medicines, news, and entertainments. Red carpet lined the corridor and there stood a palm tree. What luxury!

I was dizzy. How very far it is from one wall to the other. The nurse kept saying, "And now you walk by yourself." Would I ever be able to cover a distance like that myself? It seemed impossible. The palm tree at the end of the corridor seemed blurry to my eyes. My legs shook and felt like they were breaking under me from fear.

At that moment Taika jumped out of our ward's door and pushed me slightly with her sharp, little elbow. She raked me with a disdainful eye, proudly tossed up her head and dashed away right down the middle of the corridor on the red carpet. The little crutches thumped down the hall. From waist down to the left knee Taika was encased into a plaster corset. The hem of her nightgown swayed like a white tail. The deformed leg was a lot shorter and thinner than the healthy one. Withered and weak, it hung helplessly above the floor. The right leg stylishly hit the floor with the heel. The heel was tanned and strong. Taika could even run with the help of crutches. She put them carelessly forward, as if driving them deep into the floor, and threw her body forward. The crutches didn't touch her armpits; she walked using her arms. Her arms were strong, her shoulders wide and raised, and her neck looked too short because of it. How delicately thin it was, Taika's neck! Her dark head spun on it like a weathercock.

Oh, if only I was given crutches! I wouldn't be afraid to walk in the middle of the corridor. But without them, with nothing to lean on ... no, I can't. I envied Taika so much that I felt butterflies in my stomach. Yet Taika was bound to be lame all her life.

As early as three weeks later I was strong enough to walk freely around the ward without steadying myself on the bed backs. I no longer envied Taika. Crutches weren't the subject of my dreams anymore. And all the fear I had of Taika had gone. She even started to fawn on me. At last she promised to show to me her secret.

The entire ward had been talking about this secret of Taika's for a long time. They argued and quarreled trying to guess what it was that Taika was hiding under the blanket. She would examine it for a long time, leaving only a tiny chink for light while the entire blanket was pulled over her head. The few initiated ones kept their mouths shut for some reason, blushing and turning away when the most curious enemies of Taika tried to get it out of them.

But I had become somewhat of a stranger—not of these parts anymore. I was being prepared for discharge. I was to go to my Granny Zhenia in the far North. People said that the houses there were built from deer bones and covered with skins. In those houses lived wild people, wrapped in skins from head to foot. These astonishing things were told by the well-read people in our ward, our best authorities. They said they'd like to live in a deer bone house! They looked at me with respect, and I grew in my own estimation.

A house covered with skins was bound to be cozy and quiet, like the shed in the half-forgotten garden of my childhood. Only that shed had been under green trees. It had smelled of hay, and bumblebees had hummed inside. A house of bones and skins must be drowning in soft snow, and one would have to close the door tightly after oneself so that the snowflakes wouldn't land on one's bed.

None of us could imagine the truth. Instead of skin-covered houses, I would see fences rising up to the sky underneath several rows of barbed wire with ominous soldiers in long, stiff, sheepskin coats on top of creaking watchtowers. These towers were strange to me. They seemed to be either Baba Yaga's dwellings on chicken legs or high-mounted starling houses inhabited by forest spirits, un-doers of peaceful folk. When met on the road, these soldiers appeared normal people, fathers of children from the same school that I went to. But on the watchtowers they turned into monsters, and it was scary even to run by such a tower. *What if they shoot?*

Houses for normal people were nothing unusual, only a lot smaller than Moscow high-rises and taller than village houses.

Granny Zhenia sent me a parcel with soft boots, socks knitted of scratchy gray wool, and a fur hat and mittens from the North. The nurse brought the parcel in and undid it in my presence. I savored the scent of each thing for a long time. They smelled of a journey!

The day I was discharged, Taika, who was embarrassed for some reason, called me in a stammering voice to see "the secret." But, as it turned out, there was no secret at all—just ordinary sexual fantasies. Some of the children practiced it, others weren't too carried away by the occupation or were afraid to do something like that, because everybody knew those things were not nice, but shameful. Why they were bad and shameful, no one ever explained to us, but whoever was caught at such entertainment with herself was severely punished. This childish experimentation rose in our minds to the dimensions of a huge vice. The forbidden is enticing. Any monstrous thing is interesting because of its monstrosity.

I also tried it, but didn't become keen on the exploration of the secrets of my own body, because I was carried away by a different passion—by reading. It occupied all my time and the entire power of my imagination. I was so tired by the end of the day that I fell asleep as soon as the light went out. I even started to sleep in the "quiet hour." (Here, the dead hour was called the quiet hour so that the children would not be afraid. What if they *did* die in their sleep?)

Taika—so temperamental, so independent from the opinions of grown-ups—with her unoccupied mind, was seriously immersed in her sexual experiences. Nothing distracted her from them. But the novelty faded and she started to seek partners. Disappointed and feeling deceived, I cast Taika's blanket off my head and said out loud that there was no secret at all. Poor Taika cast a malicious glance at me, squinting her eyes that shone with tears, and turned her face to the wall. So fell her reign.

My worst enemy lay there, with her back to the entire world; a small, crippled girl that nobody expected at home. No one laid up wool socks and a smart hat for the day when she was to be discharged. No one brought her gifts. Nurses sometimes bought something tasty for her, sparing some money from their meager salaries; and we, our stomachs full of homemade offerings, let her have our jellies or cookies left over from the afternoon tea. Instead of triumph I felt embarrassment and sorrow.

ELEVEN

When it was time for my discharge, the nurses, teachers, and doctors all said good-bye to me fondly as if I were their own child. But I remember how many tortures they had to endure from me! I was disobedient. I behaved obnoxiously. Sometimes I even drove them to fury.

Would I never see the face of Doctor Vagram Petrovitch again? He had a swarthy Armenian face with bushy eyebrows. When, during my first year at the sanatorium, I gave a start and cried out from the touch of his hands during every examination, he tried to reason with me in an apologetic voice, "Have a little patience, my dear, I must know how you're getting better."

I remember him bending over me, or examining an X-ray, or walking around the ward during his everyday rounds. When his face turned to us it simply radiated kindness. Yes, he looked at us not like he looked at the grown-ups from the staff. With them he was strict and exacting. But as soon as his eyes rested upon a sick child, the frown on his brow smoothed and vanished. Even the bushes of his eyebrows seemed to get softer and his eyes shone. For us children, Vagram Petrovitch was a handsome and very important man, significant in every respect: almighty, big, strong, clever, omniscient, grand, and awe-inspiring.

Every morning before his daily rounds, nervous nurses bustled around wiping, rearranging, fanning, and checking everything for a tenth time. Vagram Petrovich demanded perfection in performing duties. Nurses checked whether the aides had done everything the way it should be done. Wearing a shining, snow-white lab coat, tall (I was so surprised later when I discovered that he was in fact rather short!) and slim, Vagram Petrovich entered the ward like a king, a white cap sitting on his unruly gray curls, cut short but still twisting like springs. Everything was shining by the time he appeared, and we lay quiet, a little stunned by the solemnity of the moment. A deferential retinue followed the king into the ward.

Some ten years later, while I was a student at Moscow University, I grabbed my camera one sunny day in fall and took the train to my old bone TB sanatorium. I wanted to take a picture of Vagram Petrovitch for a keepsake. On the ride from the station, the sun-lit asphalt road passed by long hospital buildings. I encountered grown-up patients with canes and crutches. Riding slowly by me in a wheelchair was a pale girl with stiff unruly braids adorned with large bows. She had a scarlet mouth on a sallow face. She looked at me intently. Perhaps she tried to figure out who I was going to visit. All of a sudden, things seemed unreal to me. Those subdued figures in gray hospital clothes amidst brightly colored fall leaves ablaze on the heat-radiating asphalt were alien to this festive day, a day destined for a merry and careless feast in the lap of nature. Or was the day alien to them because there was no joy in their souls to match this splendid day?

Children knew how to be joyous and to shine despite their sickness, though. They were full of anticipations of wonder. The wonder of sun, leaves and wind belonged to them in full. I realized this as I neared the well-known veranda.

Once again a wheelchair rolled by with its wheels shining and its leather peeling. The girl sitting in the chair had a deathly pale face, a face that struck the eye. I remember way back when I horribly envied a girl from our ward who was allowed to ride in such a wheelchair because she had paralyzed legs. It was the dream of all the children to have a ride in a wheelchair. You had to turn the wheels yourself, and you could go any way you liked, even spin around in one place! We thought it was much more interesting to get about like that than to walk normally on feet. Why didn't grown-ups understand? There you would go, riding in a wheelchair, the leather seat squeaking nicely, the wheels rolling against the road. And every part shining!

I ran to the veranda along the trail surrounded by familiar lime trees, birches and poplars. There was Vagram Petrovich himself, walking between the children's beds in a sun-lit aisle. He recognized me at once, and his entire swarthy face under a starched white cap smiled at me. He looked just like he had before, only his gray eyebrows didn't stick out, they hung over his eyes, like a snow-covered roof hangs over a window. I saw sorrow, care, and fatigue in his face that I hadn't seen before. And how stooped his shoulders had become.

He led me around the veranda, showing sick children to me, asking me to take pictures of them. But I realized that he was showing *me* to *them*, showing them how freely I walked, what a straight back I had. The doctor praised every child to the sky and told me about each one's particular talents. Suddenly I remembered that when I was little, he always found something to praise me for as well, and always gladly told me how fast I was recovering. He promised me I would be able to run! How I dreamed then of running across the green grass that one could glimpse from the veranda. It seemed so soft and warm, radiant in the sun. I thought grass would feel to the touch like the fur of my toy dog or like the pile of the winter blanket that shone when a ray of sun rested on it. Vagram Petrovich would show the shining lawn to me and tell me repeatedly how I would someday run across it—fast-fast-fast. I had imagined how I would fly across the grass, scarcely touching the top blades with my bare feet, so that the grass only tickled my soles.

And that had been at the time when my behavior was particularly bad. I hadn't obeyed anyone and had driven even Vagram Petrovitch to the verge of a heart attack. I'd sing at the top of my lungs during the quiet hour, right after everyone had finally settled down. An attendant on duty would come running and try to persuade me in a whisper to stop, and I'd only scream louder. Some nurse, or the teacher, or the doctor would come too. My heart would nearly stop from fear; I'd be terrified of my own bad behavior. I knew I was getting on everyone's nerves, but it was as if I was carried away by something. I'd do anything to spite the people around me. At last I was rolled out into the corridor together with my song. The entire ward furtively watched the happenings in astonishment. The little wheels squeeked, the ceiling floated above me, and I yelled all the songs I knew from start to finish. The department was small; every ward could hear what was happening in the corridor, especially in the quiet hour when all other noises had died down.

In order to keep me from exciting everyone, I'd been taken to an isolation room and left there. As the double glass doors and the solid white door of the ward had closed behind me, I was scared. I'd gone on raging for some time from fear, and then fallen silent in exhaustion, listening to the sounds outside. As soon as I heard some steps behind the door or a little rustle, I started my concert again, unless I was asleep by that time.

When people looked at me with resentment, indignation, and fury, I'd feel unhappy with myself. But it was as if something kept making me try their patience. Besides, I had thought then, *What can you do to me? I am not afraid anyway!* The sense of danger, the sense of power had turned my head. Was it perhaps my way to get even with the world for the constant feeling that I was dependent on everybody, lonely, and in pain? Did I try to prove to myself and to others that I *meant* something and had some power? Was I testing my own courage? What a joy—to drive the healthy and strong adults to the state of helplessness, their faces distorted with annoyance. I would savor my power and then calm down till the next tantrum.

John Powell, an American priest and psychologist, writes in his book *Why Am I Afraid of Loving?* of how he studied the condition of dying patients at the time when they realized that there was no hope of recovery. He distinguished phases of their behavior. The second one seems very much like what happened to me, the same furious protest: "I don't want such a destiny! I won't agree to it!" Those are the moments of an aggressive hatred towards the healthy and to those who will live on. People whose disease is grave and lingering may also be prone to these conditions. Those who nurse people in this state must be aware of this fact and be prepared to exercise patience. Perhaps that is the way the last remnants of pride burn away before acceptance can come.

There's one more explanation to the evil whirlwind that carried me when it was not in my powers to stop torturing people around me. It was a dark experience I had to go through and to understand. I was to go through other evil passions as well—malice, greed, cruelty, cravings for power. Then while I was growing up, I either turned with disgust from a familiar temptation, or if caught up in it, I would clearly understand its cost and know I had to conquer it.

The person who's gone through various trying conditions, who's known sharp falls and slow rises, who's known the fight against the whims and caprices of his own ego, can more easily understand other people who are struggling on their way through their sins and weaknesses. How can a person be free from the wicked experiences of his childhood? Perhaps only a person who grew up in an atmosphere of love, who had wise nurturers or a powerful intuition, the gracious gift of an inherently strong moral fiber—perhaps only such a person can attain freedom.

What must have been going on in the souls of the grown-ups whose lives I suddenly started to poison? They couldn't even give a smack to the obnoxious little thing because she was punished by fate already, wretched, pathetic, and crushed by sickness and hard experiences. In all this time Vagram Petrovich kept believing that I would not become embittered. He didn't stop loving me. He was glad that I was gradually growing, gaining weight, that my cheeks were getting rounder, and the dark circles under my eyes were starting to disappear.

Then years later, there I was—standing in his consulting room! In the past, a hefty nurse had carried us to this shrine. Now I saw the commonest little room, narrow, with an ordinary office-type desk, ugly chairs provided by the government, and a white couch covered with a sheet.

And the corridor that brought us there ... can it be the same mysterious, luxurious corridor with the carpet and the palm, incredibly wide and long? Was this the corridor I'd been afraid to cross? Did its walls seem then so far apart that the mere suggestion of walking from one wall to the other made me dizzy? There was the stunted palm in an old tub, the one that had been the tree of my dreams with a fluffy trunk and shining leaves. Was this the tree I had longed to walk up to and touch? To be allowed to do that, I was prepared to make an incredibly hard journey over the middle part of the carpet that heaved under my feet. The carpet seemed then so velvet-like to me that I wanted to touch it also. The windows were always full of sky and sunlight that cast cross-like shadows over the crimson carpet. It had all seemed so luxurious.

But, as it turned out, the palm hadn't received enough sun and air in that corridor. Barely alive, it had become like faded scenery. The carpet had lost its color and was balding. And the distance from one wall to the other—four paces, not more!

Vagram Petrovich, though, was even better than he had been in my memories. What a wonderful face he had! Everything in this face radiated kindness: his bushy brows, his smile, and his eyes. Even though they were not very large, they were capable of shining with tenderness, sorrow, and wisdom. I do regret that student life with its bustle and thirst for self-expression carried me away so much that never again did I come to visit this wise man. I didn't ask him more questions or tell him more about myself. The photographs, even though I had them printed, were never taken to him. They are still lying in my desk drawer.

Now, whenever I take a train and it stops at the Yauza station where our sanatorium was, I feel like getting off. I mentally run on the asphalt by the long and stocky buildings to our veranda, to the rustling trees (what a silky fresh rustle it had been!) and see the immortal Vagram Petrovich with his warm smile, walking between the children's beds in a sunlit aisle, wearing his snow-white coat and a high starched cap.

TWELVE

When Vagram Petrovich informed my family that I was almost ready to be discharged, I received a visit from Granny Zhenia. She wanted to make my acquaintance and consult with Dr. Petrovich as to what part of the country would be best for my complete recovery—the South, or the sea, or the middle belt of Russia. Depending on his answer, she was going to choose the place for us to live.

She sneaked secretly into Moscow like a smuggler, because she was forever banned from entry into Moscow and Leningrad, the capitals of the united republics, or even into any large city. She had been declared a danger for large cities in December of 1934, one day after having read in the newspaper of the assassination of Kirov. When she read about that, she said to my mother at breakfast, "How horrible political murders are! They always entail so many innocent victims." It was as if she gazed into a crystal ball! For the next day, or to be more exact, the next night, she became such a victim herself, even though she lived in Moscow, and Kirov had been assassinated in Leningrad. She was caught in the net of the Kirov campaign to hunt down enemies of the State. After five years in prison camp, and since the war was still going on, she was placed in the Komi republic in the North.

The accusation brought against Granny was "suspicion

of espionage." This suspicion arose for two reasons: firstly, because of her German last name of Herbst, and secondly, because of her five-year stay in Germany. But because of me, Granny ventured to violate the ban and came to Moscow. She feared every soldier that walked the streets. The risk was high.

Vagram Petrovich advised her not to leave the North, because the South would be harmful for me. So Granny Zhenia agreed for my sake to live of her own free will in the place where she had been in prison. She looked at me even more fondly than did Vagram Petrovich. She gazed at me full of delight, and I saw that she very much liked my eyes, my smile, my nose and eyebrows. She liked the whole of me, and all my words brought her into a state of bliss for some reason. She enjoyed every gesture of mine, every face I made, so much so that I felt that someone loved me and I was no longer alone.

I couldn't guess then that I was as lucky as Cinderella, whose godmother turned out to be a mighty fairy. My swarthy fairy, who examined me with a sorrowful tenderness, had so much warmth of soul that one could warm up on her like on a good Russian stove. All my soul was immediately drawn to her. She looked at me as if I were a jewel box that she had nearly lost forever but unexpectedly recovered and could not believe her happiness. I had no idea then how much she had suffered to be able to hold my hand and peer into my face, searching in it for the traits of her only daughter. She became my second mother. She was my support and joy till the end of her life.

I also had no idea of the desperate letters that my papa, her son-in-law, had kept sending to Granny from the front: "Take the child, save her for the sake of our Tamara's memory." But it was impossible for her to go and take me. Her German last name caused Granny to be sent to chop down trees along with other Russian Germans. She was dependent, with no passport, with no human rights, and had been unable to leave Komi to go to Siberia to get me.

I looked at my "new" Granny, who had suddenly emerged from the world of the healthy, a world unknown to me. I looked at her and wondered. Under the white smock carelessly thrown over her shoulders, Granny Zhenia wore a smart dress made of silk, not at all old-womanish. She smelled of perfume. Her hair was arranged into shining black waves. Not a single wrinkle was on her tanned face; the nose held high, the eyes shining, and all of her movements were young and light.

I always thought a grandmother was to be like Granny Brina; little, stooped, weak, with unsteady tread and slow movements. Even I, tied to the hospital bed, thought Granny Brina weaker than myself. She held my hand in hers so quietly. Because of her poor eyesight, Granny Brina's face always wore a worried and helpless expression. It consisted of a myriad of tiny wrinkles. A snow-white wave of hair was gathered at the back of her head into a tight knot. Visiting me, she always held a worn-out hand bag that she solemnly called a reticule. To be honest, that reticule was too bulky and heavy for her.

Granny Zhenia's palm was firm, her fingers were strong. She was holding a shining hand bag under her arm. She let me open the bag and have a look at what was inside. The bag had an equally shining inside that smelled of perfume. Everything in there smelled of perfume too. There was a little, white handkerchief from a fine, light fabric with a little wreath of tiny roses embroidered in the corner. There was a pince-nez in a flat case too. I had never seen a pince-nez before. Of course, I asked Granny to put it on her nose and show me what it looked like. I tried it also, but didn't see anything through the thick glass. I liked the notepad and the pencil I found there a lot better. I talked her into giving them to me. The clasp of the bag glittered like gold and gave a very loud click.

When I had enough of playing with the handbag, Granny Zhenia took my hand and told me about my mama. Her name was Tamara. She was kind, clever and joyful. When she was seven like me, she arranged a theatre in her yard and staged performances. When she mastered reading and writing, she published a family journal with pictures. She could also embroider very well, and she knitted and sewed dresses for her dolls. Granny gave me a photo of a girl with a brown bow in her hair. Then she showed me my own reflection in a little mirror. Surprise: the girl in the photograph had exactly the same face! Only I was practically bald, because my hair was cut short with clippers.

"I want a bow, too!" I said, feeling the prickly top of my head with my hand.

"You'll have everything ... ," promised Granny Zhenia, "... a bow and a dress and shiny little shoes."

How eagerly I stared at the photo of my mama. There she was, with a big bow in her hair, standing at some white wall, her thin graceful legs crossed, brown shoes on her feet. Even in the photograph, they shone brand new! Her arms were spread wide against the white background of the wall. Was she holding the wall or about to run and give someone a hug? But her eyes looked sorrowful and serious, as if she knew what would happen to her and to me.

Thirteen

During the long winter evenings in the North, Granny Zhenia told me the story of my mother's life. She gave me her letters, diaries, her school notebooks written in the archaic style, and even the family journals that she had told me about in the hospital during our first encounter.

I learned that my mother had been born in Moscow. In 1918, when she was four, her Father, a German citizen, returned to Germany with his entire family. Granny Zhenia lived in Germany for seven years. My grandfather left for Germany deathly sick already and died of diabetes two years later in a resort city of Rostock, where his mother had died before the revolution. His mother had highly praised the Rostock doctors. Although they didn't help his mother, my grandfather had hoped they would manage to stop his disease. He was but twenty-six years old.

After his death, Granny Zhenia was left alone with a child in a foreign country.

Granny told me of how the coffin with her beloved husband's body had stood in a Lutheran chapel. Candles were burning. A pastor in black spoke quietly and unintelligibly. My grandfather lay with his eyes closed, his arms at his sides and his calm, pale face turned to one side as if he were listening carefully to the pastor's words. My five-year-old mama, who was holding onto Granny's finger, whispered, "You haven't forgotten to put Papa's spectacles in his pocket, have you? Or else he'll not be able to see us from heaven, he's so blind." Granny Zhenia tried not to cry and frighten the child. ...

I begged Granny Zhenia to tell me more and more about Mama's childhood. Everything interested me, and I was ready to listen to the same stories many times over. I didn't tire of going over the photos and the exercises in penmanship or studying her letters, notes, and diaries. I wanted to piece together Mama's personality from splinters, to arrange them so that their edges fit like a jigsaw puzzle. Of course, getting to know your own mother from someone else's words is very different from the gradual learning during a lifetime together. Her papers and pictures, though, were always with me. As I grew I kept rereading them and seeing them with new eyes. At last my mother was influencing me even though she had died long ago. She was teaching me about my feelings, directing my thoughts, teaching me her attitude about people, happenings, and herself. I learned from her mistakes.

Mama knew very well what joy it was to live. When she was fourteen, she wrote in her diary:

> *Everything is so pretty, so wonderful! Laughter, air, freedom! No more fur coats, down with the last remains of winter! Spring has come! It's so nice to go to school in a tram. When windows are open, it's warm and merry. It's cozy and sunny at school too. A bell rings. Vasya enters. He says something, asks something, someone answers. But I don't see anything, don't realize anything around me. I only sense something rosy, light, wonderful ... it's the sun, the spring! I see a fly crawling on the windowsill; still sleepy and humming, it spreads its wings after*

the long and angry winter. It senses the spring too. It is glad. It enjoys the sun and happiness, and is about to dive into this sea of warmth.

The same feelings are expressed in the letter she wrote to my future father when she was nineteen:

How wonderful everything is! Life is so amazingly beautiful! I like to live so much and to feel so alive. Can there be anything more astonishing and logical than the connection between a tiny electron, the immense universe, and myself? Isn't it striking that you're the same as I? That you see the same things I see, and have the same wishes and feelings? And despite that, your belief is totally different, not like mine. And you have your own unique sense of self.

I am so surprised that Mama had such a good command of Russian at nineteen. When she was eleven, she could barely speak it and was painfully ashamed of her Russian in the first months after the return from Germany. She didn't like to go to the baker's to buy bread because she couldn't pronounce the word "bread." She kept saying instead "pread."

Another time at the butcher's she stood in line, repeating to herself the Russian word for meat. When it was her turn and the butcher asked, "And for you, girl?" she felt confused. She forgot all the words she knew and stammered out "meatishy."

"What? What?" said the shop assistant, dumbfounded.

She blurted out the well-known word, "Something!"

However, by nineteen she was very comfortable in Russian. At that age, she wrote the following in a letter describing a scientific expedition:

Bem's (that was Papa's nickname) *nose poked from the opening of the sleeping bag. The morning frost pinched it, it soon reddened and hid back into the bag. Several minutes later the sleeping bag set in motion. Puffing and groaning, it spit out first one leg, and then the whole of Bem. It happens very often that the outside differs quite a lot in appearance from the inner content. In contrast to Bem's inner orderliness, his outer appearance looked like a disorderly bundle of sweaters, padded jackets and scarves to the outside world. The bundle stamped its feet very fast, dancing a most amusing jig and waving its arms.*

Five more bundles hatched from five other sleeping bags. They were amazingly alike, each waving and stamping.

A huge rock sticks far out into the waters of the Tiberda River. The Tiberda throws its rumbling billows against it, trying to wash it away, but the rock keeps standing obstinately, defiant and trembling only a little. Sometimes the waves cover the whole of it. They must have been washing it for many hundreds of years, because its surface is smooth. The invincible rock got into a tight situation! It stands amidst the roaring, rumbling, and rushing of streams and dancing of waves. What a frenzy of energy gets crushed and thrown against it! While it only stands motionless, and there seems to be a scornful smile in its steady and calm posture.

Bem came up to me noiselessly. He stuck a cookie into my mouth and scared away my meditative mood. I might have started moping, but there were many reasons that made me change my mind. The cookie was not bad, the morning was by no means early, and Bem's looks were too comical. He'd had time to cast off several covers and remain in a torn padded jacket that gave him a hooligan look. His chin was bristly, his hair tousled, and his glasses slipped to the end of his nose.

Here is an extract from her letter sent from Moscow to Papa on expedition. He was still in Tiberda, although she had returned home:

A second-hand store opened in Torgsin. I went in to wander about and saw an amazing little foreign voltmeter. It's a little miracle! I fell in love with it at first sight. The scale was red, yellow, and blue. I wanted to buy it, but the price was 12 rubles 30 kopeks! I suffered so much!

Papa loved her with his entire being. She became half of his soul. So what was he like, Papa? My nineteen-year-old Mama described him like this:

I am with an expedition, a member of the gravimetric group. There are six of us. Bem is the boss. He is twenty-four; not tall; swarthy as a coffee bean, dark hair, dark eyes. The eyes would be beautiful were they not hidden by immense horn-rimmed spectacles, like windowpanes. Those very spectacles compensate for the over-vitality of our superior, giving him an air of distinction. Bem is very lively and hot-tempered. When he talks, his entire face is alive, his hands and whole body are alive, and it seems that even hair and glasses assume this or that expression.

Their life was full of a most interesting work they did together. They lived with the same goal. Mama was also an astronomer, and she had a great talent for mathematics. She got carried away by astronomic calculations. She talked a lot about them in her letters. It was when she went to watch a meteor shower that she met Papa.

She wrote a letter to Granny in the prison camp telling how she and Papa had been making pictures of a full solar eclipse in 1936 in a Kazakh steppe at Verbluzhia station:

> *At last the morning of the 19th arrived. At 4 A.M. we were up, excited. Bem loaded film and plates into the instruments. When a tiny slice had been eaten off the sun's right edge, we were already in the steppe with the instruments. There were fifty people there. I worked on a special device that Bem and I had designed ourselves, for determining the color of the sky in various sectors (such work has never been done before and is of great interest). When the sun diminished into a mere crescent, changes in nature around us became visible. The shadows grew sharper, the birds quieted down and prepared to sleep. The sun was growing narrower and narrower, and at the instant when it was fully covered and a bright crown set ablaze, all was transformed instantaneously and miraculously: very dark sky, bright stars, enchanting dawn spread over the entire horizon. Instead of the sun in the sky there was a black disk in a pearl halo. Four huge, red tongues, solar prominences, flamed out sharply against the halo.*
>
> *It was absolutely quiet. People fell silent from the overpowering impression; birds and gnats went to*

bed. Only the ticking of someone's watch was audible. Some time later cows from the herd stampeded into their sheds, bawling. This fantastic sight can never be forgotten. It lasted only 2½ minutes. Just 95 seconds later the moon moved on. When all coverage stages went by in reverse order, we rushed to the radio to listen to reports of the eclipse from other places. Then we sent a telegram to Izvestia newspaper ...

I'll come to visit you in two and a half months at the latest! Write me and tell me what you'd like of tasty things and gifts.

She had one year of life left. In 1936 the letter was delivered to Granny Zhenia in the prison camp in Ust-Ukhta.

Granny was lucky. She had always been fond of learning and had a pile of diplomas, attesting to her graduation from secretarial courses, courses in English and accounting. Her accounting skills saved her. As soon as she reached another halting place or a prison camp en route, she was summoned to the superiors immediately and sent to the accounting office. This was a good job even though people worked there 12 to 14 hours a day. It was in a warm place and one was sitting on a chair. These workers lived not in common barracks, but in separate rooms and sometimes even lodged with local peasants. In Ust-Ukhta the office was not in the prison camp, but in the village, and all the office staff lived in village houses.

The first time Mama managed to visit Granny in prison camp was in 1935. Granny described it to me:

In Ust-Vym the medical commission rejected me because of my heart defect. Out of two or three hun-

dred they singled out twelve weak people for the next halting station. They led us fifteen kilometers along a sandy, uphill road through the forest. On the summit we saw a most beautiful convent. Sure enough, I was sent to the accounting office at once. I was appointed the chief accountant. I felt uneasy; there were five men there already. They were all a lot older than I. Surely they must be experienced accountants. It turned out that they were barely-trained ledger clerks. The work was complicated. We worked late, till 12 at night, sometimes till 1 A.M.

One day in July, the coachman, who had been to the food warehouses in Ust-Vym, stealthily slipped me a note from Tamara late in the evening: 'We're in Ust-Vym. Can we see you?'

I sent them a note with the same coachman: 'Come with this wagon.' I went to the boss's secretary, Lafaki, a Greek. He was young, and not cruel. But still, my heart was in my mouth.

I said to him, 'My daughter is here. ... Can I see her?' He went to ask the superior, and I waited paralyzed with fear. There were fraternal relationships in the team. Finally, he came out and waved a hand and said, 'The superior gives you permission for a three day visit!'

Your mom and dad stayed with me eight days! I had to work, but the friends in the office helped. They did part of my work, allowing me to leave earlier than normal. There was a real mutual rescue system among the prisoners. Never in my later life have I known such camaraderie.

The next prison camp for Granny was Ust-Ukhta, the place where Mama visited her for the last time. While saying her good-byes, Mama promised that next time there would be three of us to visit her. She didn't suspect that her own solar eclipse was approaching, only without a pearl halo. Then in late May 1937 Mama again wrote to her mother:

> *My dear one, my lovey!*
>
> *This letter will likely reach you together with the telegram about Tatochka.* (She was sure she was going to have a girl and called me my childhood nickname even before I was born.) *I am worn out from running to and fro. So many things to do here in the house! Today I am all alone. Bem left in the morning for some godforsaken town to read a lecture there. He'll be back tomorrow morning, and go straight to work from the train. Tomorrow evening he's reading another lecture in Izmailovo, so I'll see him only at midnight! He works so very much. He took a second job as a consultant in higher mathematics and physics in the Turgenev library. Works twice in a six-day week and gets some 200 rubles. So our finances are more or less OK. At least we are getting enough for food after all that time.*
>
> *I have become so thrifty: I write down every little thing, even you can't do it like that! And still something's always lacking and can't be afforded here or there. I am idling most of the time now. I read in English a lot, study physics a bit, write articles, and that's all. Oh, yes, I have also made white slip covers for the furniture, and they turned out nicely. Now I want to embroider them. I've even found a pattern, but threads are not to be found anywhere.*

Fourteen

When Mama first gazed at me in the maternity ward, full of joy that she had a daughter now, she wasn't aware that the order for her deportation was already in Papa's pocket. The order to go from Moscow to Siberia came from the Kuibyshev regional division of State Security Directorate of NKVD, People's Commissariat of Internal Affairs. The notification read:

> *The reason for repression on political grounds by administrative order are: conviction of her mother, Eugenia Herbst, on 1 April 1935, by the Special Council under NKVD USSR, in accordance with Article 58 of the Criminal Code, for 5 years of imprisonment on suspicion of espionage.*

Having glanced at the notification, Papa dashed to Lubianka (the office of KGB, or NKVD as it was called in the '30s). He managed to convince them to put off the deportation and change the order to three weeks after she was discharged from the maternity ward. What must have been in his soul? How did he manage to conceal the anxiety, so as not to mar her homecoming?

She certainly didn't have the least suspicion. Here is the letter she wrote when she returned home:

Hello, my little 'big mama'! Today little Tatochka is ten days of age. Some say that they have never seen such a pretty baby. I am even advised to send you a telegram: 'Daughter is a real beauty!' She has very long fine hair, of a rich golden color (I'll enclose some in the letter), large eyes that are gray so far, a bow-like mouth with very red lips. She has a very beautiful face color. I'm waiting for your reply to my telegram. I don't know what name to give to Tatochka, perhaps, Zhenechka (little Zhenia)? For it is time to have her registered.

The second notice of the deportation, that by then included me as well, came fifteen days later. I was twenty-five days old. My mother had caught malaria. She was running a high fever of 40°C (104°F), with chills and weakness. She was still in the center of Moscow in summer. I read in a therapeutic reference book later that those were the symptoms of sepsis, contracted from the unsanitary work of an obstetrician.

Being sick didn't save her from deportation. Next came the hasty packing, and in such a weak and ill condition! Papa gave notice and quit all his jobs. He couldn't for a minute imagine that the deportation didn't also mean him, that he could get excluded. As long as he was not "socially dangerous" in the eyes of the authorities, he was free to leave his "dangerous" wife. She was exiled, not he.

But he loved her very much. The time came when love brought with it death. The main treasure of his life was now a threat to his life.

The author Nadezhda Mandelstam, who experienced all these feelings in full measure, comes to the conclusion: "In our life it was wiser to form no attachments. ... It's a lot harder to shatter the psyche of a lone man, it's much easier for him to keep concentrated on his own interests and lead a systematic defense."

My father felt differently, as seen in his letter to Mama: "I live for you, I breathe for you. Take my entire self. It is yours."

These confessions are very dear to me. They have been warming me for many years as they warmed Mama's heart at the time they were written. This love gave me my life, and the same love made my parents absolutely unprotected from the axe of the system that was raised over their heads. My parents were sincere in their wish to build socialism. They believed that science was to serve this system. They had worked to bring this about. But, the next thing they were doing was packing to go into exile.

I never imagined that there would be a time when I would be able to take "the file" containing Mama's case and read all the documents in the office folder. Because of the changes in our government, however, I have been allowed to read and copy her feverish, wild, naïve letter with entreaties to put off the deportation, to change the destination of Siberia for a godforsaken village where relatives lived.

21 June 1937

To: Head of State Security Directorate
People's Commissariat of Internal Affairs, Moscow
Kuibyshev District

From: Herbst, T.A., and her husband Mashbitz B.M.,
Sverchkov Lane, Bldg 10, Apt. 10

APPLICATION:

I, Herbst T.A., received today the instructions to

leave for Omsk within 5 days. I have no objections at all against the deportation itself. I only have a great request to make of you: let me go right now for one or two months (up to the 10th to the 30th of August) to a village in the Kursk region, 40 km from Elets. This request is dictated by my truly desperate situation. I gave birth to a child on the 5th of June. I haven't recovered from delivery yet. Because of some complications, undiagnosed so far, I'm running a high fever almost every day, 38-40 C. I am so weak I can barely get out of bed. ... I can't even imagine how I can physically go with a three-week-old child into a strange city without any livelihood. (At present I am dependent on my husband.) My husband can accompany me only after discharging his obligations at work. Your refusal of my request will entail the death of the child. I have a lot less milk than necessary because of weakness and anxiety of mind.

In the Meshersko-Volynskoe village, at the forest-steppe station (the Kursk region) I will be able to recover, as I have relatives there who would care for the child and for me.

I sincerely entreat you to agree to my request. Please believe me that it arises from a totally hopeless situation, and that your refusal will be equal to death for me and for my child too.

I, Herbst T.A., and my husband Mashbitz B.M., are ready to give any commitment, and after the leave—in fact, a maternity leave—we will proceed to Omsk.

My feverish situation can be confirmed by the district doctor of Chistoprudny district health care polyclinic, Comrade Shultz, who examined me. I would also like to draw your attention to the fact that I cannot be treated by medicines, as they get into the milk and can harm the child. The only method of treatment for me is rest and care.

I deeply hope that you will understand my situation and will not reject my request, and let me and my child live. I hope that you will not delay your reply, as every day of remaining in Moscow and every day of waiting are aggravating the breakdown.

T.A. Herbst,
B.M. Mashbitz, her husband.

And below the text of the letter there's a sentence added in a different handwriting:

7 July 1937

RESOLUTION:
Upon the consideration of the matter by comrade Ledens: instruct to leave for Omsk.

Ledens

Even Mama's handwriting and style reveal her hopeless despair. And someone named Ledens decided our destiny.

Many times I accompanied Papa in my mind, when he was walking with this letter first from Sverchkov lane to Lubianka and then back. I felt what must have been in his soul; how the houses and cobblestones of the street and a tram slowly crawling by turned alien in one instant, how they remained parts of the life from which he was expelled, perhaps forever. It was as if someone took a stick and broke the spine of life. Everything was in splinters. His only wish was to flee from danger, to hide his loved ones and the unprotected.

I wish they had had enough spirit to flee. I wish they

hadn't been so law-obedient. They could have called an ambulance and removed us to a hospital, or they could have secretly left for the countryside. Who would have cared to search for them? Such a desperate letter, but its pleas met a concrete wall. This was a wall where they line you up and shoot everyone without caring to look at the age, sex, or evidence of guilt.

I mourned over this letter until I realized that the Lord was merciful. He is not "Comrade Ledens." He saw what state the poor woman was in and had pity for her.

Of course, I tried to imagine Mama and Papa on their way to the destination, to the place of exile. No one was going to leave them in Omsk, a large and well-built modern city. They were ordered to proceed to the tiny town of Tara, and from there only God knows where to. I read Nadezhda Mandelstam's account of such an agonizing journey into exile. Only my parents were not by themselves, but with a child. And they had to go a lot farther than Cherdyn, the exile place of the Mandelstams.

The ordeal was too great for my twenty-three-year-old mother. By then she was diagnosed with malaria. The fever left her so weak that she could barely lift an arm or close her fingers around a spoon. I know what malaria is. I have had it too. On top of all that there was a sense of complete hopelessness, alone in a strange, cold, bleak town; homeless, without work, and in the shops ... empty shelves.

Having a baby along only made it harder. A nursing baby needs care, clean clothes and diapers, and sleep. Each nursing is such a torture when the breast skin is all cracked, swollen and discharging pus, and even the touch of the nightgown is so painful that one can barely restrain a groan. There was no way to avoid infection during the trip. So Mama suffered in a railroad car, heavy with cigarette smoke, and on the deck of a dirty, little ship before the eyes of strangers and of her husband who was tormented by his powerlessness.

After a month of the incredibly hard travel, we finally reached Tara, the town of our exile. It must have been very much like Mandelstam's description of Cherdyn: "There was a housing crisis, and the exiled were taking shelter in every corner." Every third day one had to register at the commandant's office to get a stamp on the single paper that had replaced all your other documents. The commandant "was a class war man. He always heeded his class intuition. And it never led to anything good, for how can you ever guess what it will push him to do?"

I can't imagine what it must have been like for my sick mother to wait in those queues that gathered once every three days in front of the commandant's office, where the ruler of fates, lending an ear to his intuition, decided who would live and who would die. Oh! such a queue, where one talks in a whisper and everyone is subdued and exhausted by hard living conditions, uncertainty, and abject poverty. When local citizens passed by, they would cast nasty looks at the lines of exiles. They didn't like this accumulation of unnecessary mouths in their poor town. Very likely the glances were accompanied by insults of all sorts, and maybe threats.

The Cherdyn exiles, acquaintances of the Mandelstam's, set a goal "to maintain human dignity." However, Nadezhda and Osip Mandelstam also reserved the right to give the slip to their torturers by suicide: "Thinking of this last resort has calmed me down and consoled me all my life."

This very idea started to possess Mama. It seemed to her that it was a way out! It was all the more attractive for her as she wanted to save Papa and me from the hardships of her destiny. She thought she was the rock around the family's neck that was pulling everyone towards the bottom. Her love and her pride rebelled against the pitiful fate of such a talented scientist as Papa in such a forgotten out-of-the-way place. She saw that he was going to wear himself out with working to try to feed us; that he would suffer and die. He was prepared to shoulder any burden for her, while she could not accept such a sacrifice.

Before making her final decision, she pleaded with him to leave her alone in exile, to take the child and leave while the weather was still warm, before the rains and cold winds began. He wrote about this to Uncle Vanya, who was a kind and religious person: "Leave her? I love her more than life. I can't do so mean a thing."

She sent Papa to the post office to check whether there was a telegram or a letter from Granny Zhenia or Uncle Vanya. He was afraid to leave her alone, because she was not herself. She had fits of tears and frenzy, and then she withdrew into herself and sat silently by the window. Outside, the chickens scratched in wet vegetable beds.

She cried heart-rendingly. She kept repeating, "There's a telegram waiting there, I feel it." He finally submitted and left for the post office, but halfway there he turned around and dashed back, feeling horribly uneasy at heart. He burst into the hotel room. ... But he was too late. The hasty message pinned to my blanket, read: "Go back with the child to Moscow at once! Work. Get married. Live!"

Since the very beginning of this devastating time, it was as if she were on the verge of insanity. She couldn't be left alone no matter how short a time. Then suddenly she would become calm, musing in silence. Maybe at those times her thoughts returned to an old, childhood idea of hers:

> *I love life. Strange and ungraspable, it is good beyond all measure. ... I love it even more for I don't fear it. I have the power over it, not it over me. I can stop living at any instant I choose. I am not afraid of death, and therefore I love life. Death is interesting to me. Maybe I can learn something through it. ...*

Later, my father described in a letter how it all happened:

> *Tamara's condition was aggravated by malaria with a fever of 40°C. The final stroke was this trip into exile. The psychiatrist diagnosed her with a condition on the verge of schizophrenia. During the preparations to leave she was ...*

He didn't find enough strength to finish.

Schizophrenia ... oh, the naïve Moscow psychiatrist! The Mandelstams ran across a doctor in Cherdyn who understood the matter a lot better. She gave Nadezhda Mandelstam kindly and very sensible advice: not to show her husband, that had suddenly "turned insane," to any psychiatrists and not to let him go to any medical institution. Nadezhda Mandelstam writes: "I followed this advice and was correct in doing so: *that* really disappears by itself. ... I would very much like to know what 'that' is called in proper medical terms, and why it strikes so many people under investigation."

That struck not only the people under investigation, it affected exiles as well. Sober-minded and giving in to no illusions, Nadezhda Mandelstam writes: "In such eras as ours, where is the border between a psychic norm and illness? The experienced exiles explained it to me: 'No need to worry, *that* vanishes completely. ... The illness takes from two to three months. The crucial thing is inner discipline. One mustn't try to think what will happen in the future. It doesn't promise anything good. To expect nothing and to be prepared for anything; this is the secret of balance.'"

Nadezhda Mandelstam had another secret of balance at hand: "It's so strange that we all, whether normal or crazy, never part with the hope: a suicide is the resource we always keep at hand, and for some reason we believe that it's never too late to use it."

The ones who take their own lives have the illusion that they have found a way out. The blow, however, falls on those they leave behind. A priest with vast spiritual experience told me once that suicide, in his mind, was the same as if a car rushing ahead at full speed dropped into an abyss. It's not only the driver that gets killed. Killed or crippled are the ones who happened to be next to him—his near and dear ones.

Granny Zhenia nearly died from grief. I wrote down her account of it:

> *I sent a little parcel to her: an embroidered little blouse. She loved the blouses that I embroidered myself so very much! And your dad wrote me that he had found some kind of temporary job there; they had rented a room. ...*
> *One day as I sat working at my desk, the secretary came in with the mail. I always sorted and distributed the letters myself. Hidden in the bunch of state notifications there lay a telegram. The secretary had shoved it out of sight so that I wouldn't see it at first. He gave me the entire bunch and left quickly.*
> *When I found this telegram and read it, everything went dark before my eyes. I don't know what happened to me then. I only know I said to my superior: 'Let me go home. I can't work.'*

I was let go at once. I went home and lay down on the bed. The worst thing of all was that I couldn't do anything. Couldn't go there, couldn't bury her, couldn't take you with me. Had your dad not had the idea to add to the telegram: 'She bequeathed her daughter to you,' I wouldn't have remained alive. Otherwise, whatever did I have to live for?

Fifteen

The knowledge of my mother's suicide tortured me a long time. At first I knew nothing of it, but then I started to suspect and finally knew for certain. Isn't it surprising that I love so much one who had lived before my personality was formed?

As for Papa, we had enough time together to become dear to each other. When he disappeared from my world, his love remained with me, and it grew as I grew. It changed and helped to build my world. But my love for Mama was also alive. It also grew richer and deeper.

What is it that I love? A cloud that melted away? A trace of wet inside a wrinkle? Faded photographs? Handwriting on a crumbling sheet of paper? I didn't know Mama. But something invisible has been warming, protecting, teaching, providing for me, and nurturing me all of my life.

How I wished to see Mama in my dreams! But the dreams didn't come. Once I sensed her presence. I was walking alone in the forest along a hot and dusty road. Then I lay on the grass, watching the tousled pines sweep white clouds with their tops. Suddenly I felt it: Mama was there with me! I even looked around. The grass didn't bend under her feet, the light dust on the road didn't stir, but still I felt the touch of her love and sorrow quite distinctly. I realized that I had enjoyed every moment of life for her sake also.

A whole swarm of blue butterflies was fluttering over the grass. The air was alive from the fluttering of so many wings. All of a sudden the butterflies all came and landed on my shoulders, arms, and dress. The weightless little wings quivered, opened and closed, filling me with amazement and happiness. I was afraid to take a breath, and I was thinking: "Does she see it?" and I felt that she did.

And then, in that memorable summer, I met her in my dreams. I dreamed I was in a big building that resembled the Winter Palace in Saint Petersburg, only it was not gilded and marble, but stark. The suite of rooms was full of people. The very excited crowd was waiting for something, anxious, gesturing, all talking at once. Large groups spilled from one hall into another. I was sitting on the edge of a white bench that was flat, chilly, and clean. I looked over the white walls at the immensely high ceiling and white doors thrown open wide. I looked at the mixed crowds who filled the large spaces of the halls with the humming of their voices, the pounding of their tread, and with their chaotic movement. Their anxiety and anticipation didn't concern me. I was a stranger there. No one noticed me, as if I was invisible.

Then someone sat down on the other end of the bench ... and I felt a warm wave of joy sweep over me. I looked to see who it was. And I saw Mama. *So that's what she's like—so thin and light!* Her clothes were of startling colors, a dark green skirt and a dark red blouse. Her hair was cut slantwise, falling forward in curly locks that veiled her face as she bowed her head. I rushed to her. I wanted to hold her tight, to tell her all about myself and talk of us. I physically felt the words tumbling in my throat, like a crowd of witnesses each rushing to be heard. She turned away abruptly, jumped up and dashed into the thick of the crowd. I understood that for some reason she couldn't speak to me, couldn't look into my eyes, and at the same time I sensed that her whole soul was longing for me but couldn't overcome the ban. I rushed after her. I ran across endless halls, crashing into people, getting turned about in the whirlpool of the crowd, getting pulled into the opposite stream. Fleetingly I glimpsed the hem of a dark green skirt up ahead. A lithe figure dissolved into the crowd. My heart pounded.

I begged, "Don't run away, please! I love you so much! I don't blame you for anything. For anything at all! Only give me a chance to tell you how much I love you!"

I awoke in my bed with eyes full of tears and with my heart pounding. I was short of breath as if I had been in a long and futile chase. Why couldn't she spend some time with me? She died to save me and Papa.

When Mama was three years old, Granny Zhenia took her into a church in Berlin. The child saw the crucifix. She peered into the face of Christ with its little streams of blood from the thorn wreath. She saw his hands with huge nails driven through them and started to yell and weep: "Evil people! Evil! Why have they pierced God with nails?"

Granny was worried that Mama was too sensitive and never brought her to the church again. She wanted to protect the easily wounded child's soul and didn't realize that the wounds of Christ possessed healing power. The more one thinks and cries for them, the freer and stronger one becomes, invisibly to oneself. If from childhood tears a love for Christ had been allowed to be born, maybe the whole life of the child would have taken a different course. Her character would have been formed differently, and mighty powers would have protected her from despair. Whatever might have happened to her, she never would have ended her life herself.

Sixteen

When Mama died, Papa spoke about her death to anyone who would listen, so painful it was for him. He couldn't carry this pain inside. The people around him thought he'd gone crazy and was raving. But most of all, they were scared by his fixed idea that he would dig her out from her grave and bring her back to life.

Still it was I who saved him during that first terrible time. He had to keep me in mind and take care of me all the time. I prevented him from concentrating on his pain. Ravaged by grief and fatigue, he couldn't sleep. I heard he didn't want to set me down from his arms. He looked into my face and wept. He washed my diapers in the river, having put me into some little pit that would protect me from wind.

Whenever I look at the waters of a large river, I almost see Papa bending towards the stream with its swift current, wet breath, and many voices murmuring, splashing, rustling. The river has a goal toward which it rushes with unflinching determination. To watch this well-directed motion is healing for the soul.

Perhaps it was there on the Irtysh River that he suddenly felt he had found hope that everything could still be changed. Long ago when he was a lecturer at the Moscow Planetarium he laughed at the ideas of that weird philosopher Fedorov that humankind was to bring back to life all the dead ancestors and build a new life on the planet together with the risen. And Tsiolkovsky propagated the idea that strength of feeling was an unbroken staircase, descending from the living world into dead matter. The staircase went beyond the border of life. Might the strength of feeling of the living bring the dead to life again?

In Stevenson's "Owner of Ballantrae" the Indian, Sekundra, dug his master out of the grave where he'd lain for several days, and tried to bring him back to life. He failed for only two reasons: the air was too cold, and Ballantrae was a scoundrel. Papa recalled how Mama had read Stevenson in English when expecting me in those peaceful days of spring. What a great happiness to read without haste, to fear nothing, to look at each other in a clean and cozy room of your own. She was reading Stevenson and translated for him this horrible passage straight from the page. Afterwards they talked a bit about the ideas of Fedorov and Tsiolkovsky, ideas which seemed to Mama and Papa so detached from life, so artificial, total balderdash.

Now Papa dreamed of meeting such a man as Sekundra and finding out the method for revival. He continually thought about it, imagined how he'd learn the method, dig up the coffin, tear off the lid, see her face, and bring her back to life. The decay would stop and go backwards! Life would return to her, fill her, and her life would continue. He pondered this idea again and again. The idea became the dream, his cherished dream. However, his friends in Moscow listened to him with pity, nodded, expressed their compassion, and became more convinced in their belief that he'd gone mad.

Our way back to Moscow had been very long. Papa sent cables to the heads of landing-piers and train stations en route, saying he was carrying an orphaned baby and asking for help to find a wet nurse. Women who lived close to the stations we passed through came to the steamship or to the train and nursed me. My life consisted mainly of sleeping, but the brief times when I was awake were filled with contrasts: feelings of hunger, thirst, cold, of being nasty wet and of blissful dry, rest and a full stomach. If parents let strangers come near their baby and they treat it only with kindness, warmth and tenderness, it grows up friendly and trusting.

Papa now regarded as a friend every woman with a baby. He could simply come up to a nursing mother and hold out his baby. No explanations were necessary. One glance at his face was enough, and the woman understood without words that he'd been bereaved, and took me and put me to her breast once her own baby was satisfied. Papa watched me grasp with a greedy mouth at the nipple of a strange woman, and he wept without noticing his tears. Nanny Dasha told me about it. I have so many foster brothers and sisters along the Irtysh and on the stretch between Omsk and Moscow. They are of different nationalities, of different faiths, of different customs. They nursed me in the literal sense of the word; I owe my life to them. I can't prefer one nationality over another. Every mother's milk is like the water of life in a Russian fairy tale; it brings life.

Pressing me closer to him, Papa cherished his dream, and maybe he whispered something about Mama as he peered into my face. Just eight years later I longed as fervently to bring him back to life, as I stared at his face in a little crumpled photograph.

SEVENTEEN

Papa had a room in a communal apartment on Sverchkov Lane, shared by several people, even families. On his return to Moscow, he went to work at a school teaching astronomy, physics, and mathematics. He was no longer allowed to engage in scientific work, for he'd compromised himself by following his suspect wife into exile.

There are some memories of this time that still stay with me. I remember waking up after a childhood illness and feeling my strength returning to me. I felt like running over the warm parquet floor to the window, climbing onto the round seat of a wooden armchair, then onto the writing desk, onto its green blotter—a vast meadow with a dark ink pot of marble and bronze.

Beyond the desk was the window. Through the window one could see a gray yard with a single dusty and crooked lime tree in the middle. Of course I didn't mind the dust. I noticed, though, and remembered it later. Really, what is dust, when the leaves are green? And when the sun shines through them! The shadows that ran across the sand in the sandbox were just like the shadows on the large boulevard of Chistye Prudy, where Nanny used to take me for a walk.

I was glad the lime tree was crooked! It meant I would be able to climb it some time in the future! I would sit on a branch somewhere high, and look far around—even though there was nothing but windows, windows, and more windows of all the tall buildings all around.

Downstairs there stood big trash containers with half-closed lids. Old newspapers and rags stuck out from under the lids. Little tufts of dusty grass peeked from under the cobblestones.

Things seemed almost magical. I thrilled to touch them. The papers smelled of antiquity, the dresses smelled of shop. The chairs were prepared to gallop on their curved legs, the sofa was ready to sail across the parquet sea. And the curtain over the windowsill was curved like a sail full of wind.

After a whole kaleidoscope of nurses and nannies, I got Nanny Dasha. I came to love her—her face, hands, hugs, little words, and the warm smell of her hair and dresses.

Children have different measurements for time and space. A whole era passes from breakfast to lunch, from lunch to dinner, and an entire universe fits into the space between the door of a room and the window. All things there are alive, just like people, and have their own interests. They can change their aspects. The curtain hanging over the bookshelf can sway maliciously in the twilight, threatening to let out something horrible that will fill my entire soul with fear. Other times it kindly conceals me in its dusty folds when guests are taking off their overcoats, laughing and talking loudly in the anteroom, and I have a severe attack of embarrassment—so severe I could cry.

I remember childish fears. The fear of putting my legs down from the sofa. *What if something jumps out from under it, something flat and dark? What if it jumps out and grabs me with its paws?* I made short dashes from chair to chair with their round backs and round seats. I very much liked to spin on them. The wooden arm-rests hugged me firmly, protecting me from falling to the floor, and every chair was a secure little fortress.

In the corridor beyond our tightly shut door there transpired a totally separate life: steps, voices, and telephone calls. Sometimes the front door would bang, and one second later my white door would fly open, and Nanny Dasha would appear, flushed and smelling of the city wind and rain, with a heavy bag hanging from her elbow. That bag always contained some tasty treat. Other times I would sit gazing at the white door with entreaty in my eyes, but the door remained motionless. When Nanny Dasha wasn't there, all the things kept silent and waited. They wanted to be still for a while without people.

Papa's bed was so grand! It was the proud owner of shiny ornamental balls, which were always cold, sticking on the headboard made of rods and cross pieces. A simple white bedspread lay so solemnly on the bed. I felt I mustn't crease it. Just let me try to climb on the bed without permission, and that cover would give me away at once! The pillow was set upright, in a triangle with one corner pointing up. The pillow knew all Papa's night dreams and thoughts. Its soft ears stuck out, and I would whisper my wishes into them, so that it could convey them to Papa.

My own little bed with a protective net was in the corner behind the wardrobe. It looked mysterious in the daytime. It was chilly and dark inside the net. I felt like climbing in and playing there, but I knew I mustn't. The bed was only for sleeping. Each time I went to bed, I gazed for a long time at a small wall rug with three dwarfs under a red mushroom. It smelled of glue and canvas. The dwarfs peeked cunningly from under their hoods, pulled almost over their eyes. This rug was a remnant from my mama's German childhood. She also used to fall asleep under it.

Many things there were Mama's. The slipcovers on the armchairs, the sofa cushions, and the teapot cover were all embroidered by her hands.

But Mama was no more, and I had Nanny Dasha instead. She had her own children and always yearned to stay with them. But she always kissed me when she put me to bed, always cajoled me into eating one more spoon of semolina, consoled me when I quarreled with children in the yard or when I had a bump. If I became ill she'd sit by me and hold my hand. She'd give me medicine or put a cold compress on my forehead. She talked to me about her children, about life in the country, about the piglet Vaska and the cow Lyubimushka.

Before the war I spent every summer with Granny Zhenia's brother, Uncle Nikolai and his wife, Elena Vladimirovna, that I called Antalesia, combining Aunt with Olesya. They lived at a forestry experimental station that stood on the border between the Tula and the Orel regions. My uncle, Nikolai Vekhov, was a deputy director for science there. This was the place to which my mama had implored the unyielding Comrade Ledens to let her go.

They had a house there with a grand piano, flower beds under the windows, and a garden. Elena worked at the station for a time, but then turned into a full-time housewife as the work around the house required much time and effort. She had many people to feed. Besides her own family, which consisted of herself, her husband, her two sons, and her sister, there were also the visiting station staff and graduate students who worked there under the tutorship of Nikolai. They all dined with us. By then Uncle Nikolai had been promoted to professor, the highest rank a university teacher could hold.

To buy food, they traveled to the nearest town, Efremov, on horseback or by car.

I loved Aunt Elena. One time she wrote about me to Granny Zhenia in the prison camp:

> *At last the little one is at our place. ... She came with her papa and her nanny. ... We have a lot of flowers, and this year I've arranged the beds properly. We've roses, peonies, carnations, and what not. And you know, when someone holds out flowers to the little one, she doesn't sniff at it, but exhales through the nose and clicks with her tongue as if to say, 'How tasty!' Well, as for Nikolai Kuzmich, our father, he has grown old, his face thin, and so many gray hairs.*

The house was always merry and full of joy. They organized home festivities, soirées, and concerts. Aunt Elena put a lot of imagination and originality into them:

> *I arrange concerts fairly often. We celebrated because Volodya* (the Vekhov's younger son and my mom's cousin) *passed the entrance exams and was now a freshman at the biology department of Moscow State University. We gave him a pine tree with honey cakes hanging all over it, and suggested he breed a new sort of tree (pine honey-caked), and on a festive table I served a dish: pink islands in a milky lake (cherry mousse with milk) and told Volodya to build a country of islands like that. Tomorrow we'll likely have dancing with various lighting effects: I have five or six strips of cellophane of different colors. I'll put colored screens in front of the lamp. ... Some time ago I had a Grieg soirée, with*

quotations from his biography. There was another time we had an evening of music, and of course I played nocturnes. Such are our entertainments. ... And now I'm busy about the house all day long, and often there's not a spare minute to play the piano, so my technique has dropped considerably. Well never mind, I'll play in winter.

Aunt Elena also wrote of how she took care of me.

If she falls, we don't sympathize with her. We advise her to get up and check in which part of the floor she has made a hole with her nose.

I still remember a stretch of the floor painted yellow that I scrutinized very thoroughly. I remember how cool, clean, and even it was. I think I must have been very much impressed by the thought that I was not the only one who was hurt, and that I could really have made a hole in the floor. I touched my nose with my finger and found out it was soft only on its tip, while inside it was hard! It could easily poke a hole in this floor. *Can the floor really be hurt? How can I find out? Unfortunately, it never cries.*

Aunt Elena wasn't afraid to send me on errands, though I was only two. She trusted me to carry things, to take something to somebody, to return things back to their place; and I set off to perform the task with joy in my heart. There was a vast flower bed next to the house, and I had my own little garden. I planted sticks and was sure they would turn into flowers. A trail was cleaned and covered with yellow river sand for my sake. I drew big black scribbles on it, for the soil was black under the sand. I had a hammock of my own. It was hung close to the earth so I could reach it with my feet and I could swing myself.

Aunt Elena wrote to Granny Zhenia:

> *She says, 'My hammock.' She has a little bench of her own. Once, sitting on her little bench, she glimpsed smoke rising from the chimney, and was especially impressed by the fact that it had something to do with the samovar. I'm with her 24 hours a day. I manage to scrape up a few minutes to do some fancy work (I didn't get rid of that passion) but there is no way I can play, as the rival won't tolerate my music. She finds she can play a lot better, and starts to slap the keys with her fingers straight away. It took me quite some time to understand what 'Antalesia, piaai' meant. It turned out she wanted to play the piano.*

It was under Aunt Elena's grand piano that I sat and listened to her play. My thoughts returned to her playing later during the evacuation and in hospital. Then I remembered it as the dearest and the most wonderful experience in my life. The music rumbled and droned in every board of the floor and inside myself, and curious trees and bushes walked up to the wide open door, peeped into the brightly-lit rooms, and softly sighed. I both wanted and feared to walk towards them, to step over the border between the indoor light and the outside darkness.

I was at Aunt Elena's when the war began. Everyone feared that some paratroopers would suddenly appear. Of course I didn't understand who they were. I thought they must be horrible monsters if the adults were so scared of them. We started to wander from place to place, to flee from bombings.

For some reason we moved into a shed, where I sincerely enjoyed the company of the pig, sheep, and chickens, and didn't suffer from flea bites as did the grown-ups. I turned into a country child. I mothered a small log swaddled in a rag, calling it my little daughter.

What I don't remember, I learned from the letters Aunt Elena wrote to Granny Zhenia, which she kept. They painted a vivid picture of our life and the chaos of the evacuation, the insanity of sudden preparations to leave. She told of the ravaged home and the grand piano left behind like a doomed being in the forsaken house.

Vividly I remember Papa's face. As soon as he removed his glasses, his face ceased to be grown-up. To me, being adult meant being strong. Grown-ups were the people who could do anything and knew everything, and no one would dare to hurt them. But as soon as Papa took off his glasses, he turned into a boy who had just been knocked off his feet. Yet he still remained so big compared to me that I had to throw back my head to look at him.

I wonder how he ever managed to persuade the military commissar to accept him for the army. He was so nearsighted he wasn't even fit for the volunteer corps. But as the fascists moved closer and closer to Moscow, he became restless with worry and a thirst for action.

I remember how he walked with me around the city that no longer resembled its former self and how he squeezed my hand in his whenever a volunteer corps or soldiers marched discordantly past us. He always paused by the placards emblazoned with "What have you done for the front?" and "Motherland calls." The woman in the posters had a harsh and frightening face with hideous strands of hair and that accusing finger pointed straight into my eyes.

In shop windows, thick-bellied sacks of sand replaced the handsome mannequins with their pleasant smiles and glassy eyes. Where did the mannequins go? I had always dreamed of having such a life-size doll to dress up and put into bed. Where had those "dolls" gone? I wished they had given them to little girls.

There was nothing to look at! How boring! There were no people strolling in the streets. Now everyone rushed everywhere. Passersby had a troubled look; even their clothes were no longer fashionable or interesting. A volunteer unit turned onto an empty lane from behind the corner, singing a discordant ditty. It was so bizarre to see these people making efforts to march evenly in a formation. They were not servicemen at all, just men like my papa. He stiffened on the dusty cobblestones, looked at them through his glasses, and where was his joyful smile? He was nervous, in a hurry, he dragged me along, and I was afraid. I ran stumbling after him.

I can't imagine what he was like in action. I am a lot less nearsighted than he, but without my glasses I see a blurry spot instead of a human face at a distance of three paces. I was told that his rifle had been an old-fashioned one from 1913. It very likely recoiled hard against the shoulder when fired. At school I shot from a light rifle, and it sprang back quite considerably. I always had to grab my glasses. In war, glasses must be a complete hell to their owner. They either fog up and you have no way you can wipe them, so you walk blindly; or they fall off when you stoop in a jerky movement; or they grow dirty. One has to think of them all the time and take care of them.

Papa could have left the volunteer corps. His unit lived in some school in Moscow for quite a long time. It must have been somewhere near our house, because Nanny and I simply walked there on foot to visit Papa and to take him food.

Afterwards I wanted for a long time to get into that school yard scattered with hay. I remember tired volunteers sitting on hay next to Papa. The wind drove the hay all over the lane; its yellow scraps chased us for a long time as we left. Papa peered after us through his glasses. I kept looking back and we waved to each other. In the evacuation I recalled those people sitting on the hay in the schoolyard and my Papa standing by the fence, and I thought, *What if he's still standing there?*

The volunteer unit gradually fell apart. People wearied of their initial heroic impulse and started to assess their abilities and circumstances soberly. What kind of warriors would they make with their chronic diseases, with the burden of age, with their antiquated rifles to fight against tanks and machine-gunners on motorcycles? Someone got a job at a plant, someone at an office. My papa could have left, too. A friend of his dropped by and suggested to him to leave and go into the scientific reserve, which was necessary for the defense.

But Papa replied, "If I was Russian, I would do that. Afterall, what kind of soldier am I, with my eyesight? But I'm a Jew! I don't want to bear the reproach that a Jew hid behind the back of the Russian soldier. I'd rather die in a battle." He looked at things quite soberly and was sure he'd die. My papa's friend, on seeing Papa in military uniform was taken aback and his heart ached, he told me later. Papa was not at all a belligerent soldier. He had a thin neck in the wide collar of the field shirt. He wore powerful, heavy spectacles on a pinched face. Everything was sized too big for him, from the boots with puttees to the field shirt. Only the forage cap was too small; it barely covered his large head.

As for me, only eighteen months after Papa had joined the volunteer corps, I became ill with TB. I kept dreaming in my plaster bed of how Papa would come back and I'd instantaneously recover, how he'd take me from hospital and we'd be happy. I kissed his little photo in the daily quiet hour, pulling the sheet over my head so that nobody would interfere. I begged him not to die, but to return to me. Maybe I made him my god for a certain time and prayed to him. This icon of mine was a little document photo. It was a bit out of focus and it got yellow along the edges, with a crack that went right across the entire face—from the forage cap to the field shirt collar that was too wide for him.

A sorrowful face with sunken cheeks looked from the photograph. I kept this scrap of photographic paper as my guarantee that Papa was alive and he would come back. There he was looking at me as if he wanted to tell me something! I kept waiting for him when his body was already mixed with the clay of the Rzhevsk lands. He remained alive only in my memory. When I realized that there was nothing more to wait for, I imagined myself searching for him at the battlefield and bringing him back to life with the help of the water of life.

So clearly did I imagine us walking around Moscow together again, that later when I grew up, those imaginings seemed real happenings to me. The imagination is based on reality. Some memories seem like yesterday, others are as faded as my photograph. Once upon a time, long long ago ... did it all really happen? Did we really sit together on some carved stone stairs heated by the sun? Did the river splash at our feet, the clouds float above in the blindingly blue sky? Did the shadows and light alternate on his smiling face, constantly changing it? Did the balloons sway on long threads overhead, knocking into each other with soft rubber thumps ... ?

I do know that I had every reason to be proud of Papa. He was ennobled by a halo of heroism: he was a soldier! A Motherland Protector! The radio sang of such people. The announcers and teachers talked about them in solemn voices, not at all embarrassed by their enthusiasm. Even many years later I was sometimes drawn into this kind of military patriotism.

I loved to watch Papa shave in the morning. He swept his chin swiftly with a soapy brush, and in a couple of whisks he turned into a clown from a circus, with a white chin. You only had to paint on a merry red mouth. But Papa made me laugh without anymore makeup. He swirled soap first on one cheek, and then another, so as to scrape the foam off them together with the bristles. His mouth twisted first to one side, then to the other. I was delighted and beside myself with laughter. By noon Papa's cleanly shaven cheeks were prickly again. I loved to brush my palms and face against his bristles. These prickly cheeks were manly, virile. I'd press closer to the prickly cheek, and nothing in the world would frighten me!

After he was gone if I heard some child yell "Papa!" and dash to his papa with his arms widespread so as to jump right into a hug—then I ran away and hid to have a good cry in quiet without witnesses. What did I know of my father? What can a child of four or five know about her parent? I remembered that he'd been kind, strong, and merry. When he hopped about the room with me on his shoulders, he laughed as much as I did. I would be laughing and squealing, grasping his thick mane of hair, trying to balance. When he reached the lampshade with fringes, which hung like an orange from the ceiling, he liked to jump up to let me touch the fringes.

When I grew up a bit, I learned that my papa was an astronomer. Granny sent me several easy brochures on astronomy so that I could understand what it was. She wanted me to learn to find answers to my numerous questions myself, so that I'd quit bothering other people with them. I read those brochures when I was still in my plaster confinement, and they shaped my imagination. They spoke of white, blue, yellow, and red stars. They talked of Mars, where, with the telescope, one could discern stripes that looked like canals dug by some mysterious creatures; and of explosions on the constantly boiling sun; and of Earth flying in a black emptiness around the sun, like a ball on a thread.

After five years in plaster I forgot what the night sky looked like except for the view from the window. Then a small scrap of memory floated to the surface of my mind. ...

> *An aircraft warning was sounding. We were running along a dark lane. I was sleepy, hastily dressed. I kept stumbling in my unlaced shoes. I didn't want to run, though something rumbled somewhere very close. And all of a sudden something tossed me upward, and I fell down with my back against the cobblestones; the pain was so sharp that my breath stopped for some seconds. I was lying on my back and seeing gray clouds over the rooftops, and dark gaps between the scraps of clouds. There were long white smoking blades of searchlights, running over the clouds and the blackness.*

After my release from the hospital I would climb out on the roof of Granny Zhenia's house on a blue evening in fall and look at the sky. I lay on the warm shingles and watched the crescent moon get brighter and brighter and the stars shine clearer and clearer in the darkening blue, and I was filled with delight. This majestic picture was living. It kept changing all the time. Clouds were running between me and the stars. The blackness, where stars shone brighter and brighter, was getting more and more fathomless. It turned out not at all velvetlike. It was giddily empty, eerie, and yet extremely inviting and fascinating, like a secret you cannot unravel.

It's a pity that I didn't know the names of the stars. I didn't have a map of the sky. But I knew that every star had its own destiny. It first lived through its childhood, then through youth, maturity and old age. I tried to tell from their color and twinkling which star was still a babe, which was a grandmother. Papa knew the secrets of stars!

Later, Papa's sisters told me that he'd been longing for the sky since he was three. On starry nights he climbed trees to take a closer look at the stars. When he was six, he suddenly disappeared and was absent all day. He returned hungry, scratched all over, but very proud of himself. He had made an acquaintance with a pilot on a big field outside the city limits where one tested aircraft and people could buy admission tickets to go for a ride into the sky. So as not to scare the spectators and to convince them the attraction was safe, the pilot flew into the sky with a small child—with my papa. The pilot called him "Sonny." From that day on Papa dreamed of flights to the stars and often discoursed on the subject, entertaining the adults enormously.

I have a book on meteorites that Papa wrote together with a pal of his who later became an academician. The book is over enthusiastic, as was characteristic of the style common in books and articles written in the '20s. It was the style of the proletarian cult, of the belligerent atheists, a hooligan over enthusiasm, that always thrust the writer's opinion on the reader. It is the attack of a subverter, one who's so much carried away by the passion of overthrowing things that he's incapable of taking in someone else's thought or idea.

Papa was carried away by the desire to explain everything simply, easily, and mechanically. In his letters to Mama, Papa was entirely different, clever and reasoning soundly. Where did all those qualities hide when he was writing his book? The temperament of an atheistic preacher suppressed all. The book lists proofs that there is nothing mysterious in meteorites; they are common splinters of common heavenly bodies. He propagated the commonness of astronomy so passionately, trying to prove that it was as clear a sphere of human knowledge as chemistry or biology. He preached it so passionately, that astronomy became ... poetry.

One cannot love a commonplace, thoroughly prosaic occupation so passionately. So it seemed that he tried to unmask the mystery with such a rage because actually he was impressed by this mystery, by the incomprehensible world, where behind every revealed secret you sense the contours of further ones. But they slip away from you and you've no idea how to unravel them.

Papa, who loved the sky, instead went to the war front with the volunteer corps. I, however, found myself on a train with the evacuated people, then in a Siberian outpost, and from there with an old woman who gave me shelter in her cabin in a village near Alapaevsk. It was there that my Aunt Leah, Papa's sister, discovered me dying from the bone tuberculosis and malaria. It was Aunt Leah who found a place for me in a hospital in Sverdlovsk. She wrote of it to my papa in a letter that came too late for him to receive, and to Granny Zhenia in the prison camp. Granny Zhenia kept all her postcards. Here's one of them, of 4 January 1943:

> *Dearest Eugenia Kuzminichna!*
>
> *Little Marianna is in a bone TB sanatorium. The back and sacrum are in a plaster cast. She'll have to lie like that for some two years. It's evident you cannot take her to live with you, for she must con-*

tinue the treatment. When the process is stopped, she'll have to wear a corset for six years. ... I visit her on Sundays; she's just 5 km from me. She's gained some weight compared to what I'd seen in the village.

It was 1944 when Aunt Leah returned to Moscow and transferred me into the children's bone TB sanatorium by Moscow. Aunt Elena was back from the evacuation, too. She came to see me in the sanatorium. Afterwards, she wrote:

Dear Zhenia!

At last I have seen little Marianna. How frightening it was to lose sight of each other on the roads of war. Now I can visit her and watch her recover and grow. ... In summer the children live on a walled veranda. She was rolled out to me in her bed. ... Her arms are so little, so thin, the little face is browned by the sun. The chin is sharp like Tamara's, the eyes are dark. She told me proudly she was already seven and could read, and when she recovered, she'd go to school. She showed me her toys. ... Her head rests not on a pillow, but on a folded towel. ... I brought her a buttered bun, she started to devour it, but couldn't finish it all, so we left it for later, and she looked over the cookies and chocolates—and the rest we entrusted into the nurse's keeping, and we wrote on the bundle "Little Marianna."

I asked her—did she ever cry? It turns out she does, when boys offend her. I advised her to press her hand into a threatening fist and thrash them as they deserve, and taught her to make a fist. She asked did

I remember how I saved a girl who had cut her little leg with a scythe, and much blood had poured out of the girl's leg!

She clutched at my dress (the white yoke attracted her attention), tried to wriggle my briefcase from me. I promised to get her pencils and paper—they are always short of those things. I kissed every finger, each cheek. ... 'Does your little back ache?' I asked her. 'Well, it does,' she says, 'but not much, and before, in a different city, it ached a lot.' She's lying in a plaster trough like the ones babies are weighed in. She's tied to the bed all the time. She didn't want to let me go, but it started to drizzle, and I rushed off, having promised to come back.

Oh, how I wanted to rush off with her into her wonderful, festive, active and moving life! Why don't the people who can walk—and even run—realize how lucky they are? When I learned to walk, up in the North, and entered a forest for the first time, a feeling of awe and delight filled my soul. The giant pines and birches seemed to me mysterious creatures, chained to their place, so that they didn't fly away and leave the soil bare. Their cloud-like tops and string-like trunks all rushed upwards toward the sky. I thought the trees were spellbound by their wish to fly, as strong as my passionate desire to walk. They must want to fly, for various winged creatures live on their limbs—birds and insects, and the wind that sweeps across vast open spaces sways their giant bodies, and the clouds fly by continually.

Whatever is happening down by the roots is so far away and insignificant compared to what the tops feel, that the trees must be barely taking notice of it. So I stood, small and still, knee deep in the wet grass at dusk, barely breathing with delight, afraid to take a step for fear that I might kill something quite tiny on the ground.

These memories I stored in the fading scrapbook of my mind to take them out occasionally and sort through them.

EIGHTEEN

Even as an adult, every time I thought of Mama's death, a hopeless pity would ravage my soul. I started to pray. I simply asked God to warm her soul, take her to Him, pity her, forgive her. Just as physical pain obeyed prayer and vanished in my childhood in the hospital, now the pain of my soul was no longer as stinging. I felt that prayer was changing something in me and around me. I sensed some warm contact, as if prayer was a bridge thrown across the abyss of time and space.

I wasn't a real believer. Like everyone does when circumstances push them out of the common norms and needs, I had pondered about faith, about the sense of my life. I started my prayers with these words: "Lord, Creator of the world, if you really exist and if you hear man ..."

My thoughts ran like this: *Suppose that beyond the grave, there is nothing. Then my prayer has no meaning whatever; then it is simply some means to comfort myself. And yet what if there is? For two thousand years people have been praying in churches 'for the repose of the soul.' What is it then? An age-long custom—a dark, but extremely survivable delusion? If there's a tiniest possibility that prayer is heard, then how could I refrain from it?*

I decided I must have a funeral service performed in a church for Mama. *But how does one do that?* I wondered.

Is an unbaptized person allowed to enter the church? In my search for faith, I recalled my days in the hospital. The women often talked of how a church prayer helps the souls of the dead, and how necessary it is. Here's one account:

> *An old and frail woman came to the priest and entreated him, 'Go to a certain man, take his confession, give him the Eucharist. He's about to die.'*
>
> *The priest said, 'I've no time right now. Give me the address. I'll go there when I'm done.'*
>
> *She gave him the address written on a scrap of paper. He finished the ceremonies and set off. He pressed the doorbell. The door was opened by a young man with a healthy, rosy complexion. The priest showed him the note. 'Does this man live here?'*
>
> *'Yes.'*
>
> *The priest entered and asked, 'Are you the sick one? Is it you I must give the Eucharist to?'*
>
> *'Me? Oh, no, I'm quite healthy, and an atheist too.'*
>
> *'A woman came to call on me. She left me a note with an address. Here it is.'*
>
> *'A woman? But I live all alone.'*
>
> *The priest glimpsed a photo on the wall and recognized the old woman. 'But there she is! She came to me and left this address.'*
>
> *'Impossible! She died 18 years ago when I was still a boy. That's my grandmother.'*
>
> *'And the handwriting, is it hers?'*
>
> *The man dug in a drawer and extracted a creased letter. They compared it to the note. It was the same hand! The amazed priest described the old*

woman in detail. The man was very troubled and upset.

He said, 'Well, it's all so bizarre. Now I feel scared and I don't know why. Please take my confession and give me the Eucharist.'

Well, the priest took his confession, gave him the Eucharist and left. Early the next morning, the man stepped out of his house, was run over by a car, and died. His relatives brought him for the funeral service into that church, to that priest whom the old woman had visited.

His grandmother, she must have prayed a lot. Her prayers were heard.

Here's another story that was told:

It's no good to cry over the dead, it's harmful for them! We had a little sister, Dushka, who died. We cried and cried, and kept recalling her memory. Once when we were sitting on the porch, and happened to glance at the rug Dushka had woven, we were heartbroken and wailed aloud. Suddenly we heard her voice from over the fence, 'Hey, stop crying! You've drowned me already!' We looked up and saw her two hands on the fence, but she wasn't seen, as if hiding behind the fence.

Another story went like this:

My daughter-in-law had a dream. In that dream her husband, who had drowned some time before, said to her, 'Really, I don't know if I should leave our son with you or bring him here.'

When she awoke the next day she was very troubled. She was not herself all day long and was very uneasy. She waited to see what would happen and didn't let the child out of her sight. Then, somewhat later, there appeared a little black spot on the boy's leg. Gangrene set in and he died three days later.

Yet another story:

Our Nina's father died, and she wept for him. She had a dream about him. He was lying dressed in the clothes he had been buried in, in a bathtub full of clean, clear water. The old women interpreted the dream for her. 'He was drowned in tears. One mustn't weep so much for him. It is better to pray for his soul.'

'Oh, yes, yes,' said another. 'It was exactly the same with my daughter-in-law. She wept for her little boy such a long time and kept asking God, 'Lord, let me see my little boy, if only in a dream!' Her prayers reached God.

So she dreamt that she was walking through a long corridor, and suddenly a door opened in front of her. She saw a large room ahead and many, many children in it. They played and ran around the beds.

'My son's not here,' the mother said, casting a glance over the children, and went further. Again a door opened, and again she saw a room, even bigger than the first one, and also full of children, and her son wasn't there either. Only in a third room she found her little boy. He was wearing what he had been buried in. He took his mother to show her his bed. 'And here, Mama, is where I live now.'

She watched him take a sugar cube from under the pillow and start to nibble on it. She asked, 'Who's bringing you sugar here, honey?'

'You. When you remember me down there, something is always brought to me here.'

His bed was a good one, but wet. 'And why is your bed wet, dear?'

'Because you weep for me too much, Mama.'

Why did I write down all these stories? It seemed to me I should gather it all: revelations and speculations of philosophers, experiences and tales of common people. Then when it was all gathered in, the puzzle would fit together and the picture become clear. I wanted to understand what had happened to my parents, what their deaths meant.

Through the ages it has been taught that you should have a funeral service for the ones who were baptized. Mama was baptized. But what about me? Had I been baptized? How could I find out?

"Since I don't know," I decided, "I'll go to a church and have myself baptized."

Why baptism was necessary, I had no idea. Even much later, when I was a believer, I kept thinking, *If I am convinced that God exists, that he loves me, and if I feel that I love him, then why should I be baptized? I talk to him in my prayers, and he answers me. He knows I have come to care for him more and more and think only of him. I am like the man from the Gospel parable of the person who found a large pearl. I rejoice that I have found the real treasure of my life! Surely he knows I am grateful for his every attention with all my heart.*

Yes, but people have been baptized for two-thousand years, and, most important, Christ himself asked John to baptize him! Christ himself! Asked to be baptized!

"Well, it's decided," I said. "I'll do it, and I'll try to find out later why it's necessary! What's more, if our Soviet authorities persecute people who get baptized or married in church, or who go to church, that means they fear it. And that means there's truth in it.

I lingered thus on the church threshold a long time, not having enough courage to enter, and not sure whether the temple was Temple for me. For I was alone in my search, with no guide. As an adult I spent time in a hospital once again with tuberculosis of the hip joint. One of my fellow patients secretly gave me her Gospel, a little booklet printed illegally in small print on very thin pages. One Gospel had already been taken away from her and she was afraid she'd lose this one. She went to the restroom to read it. She also prayed there. For you could bolt the door from the inside, and if steps sounded near, the book disappeared into the pocket of her gray hospital gown.

To find myself a place to read, I used the tricks of my childhood and arranged a reading hall under a white sheet, pulled over me like a tent. I read in my white tent, and it was not just reading, but walking into faith. I perceived every word like a story of the things that had happened to Him who loved me. I was especially moved by the passage where Peter, who disowned Christ three times, heard the rooster crow, left the courtyard with its fire and wept bitterly. My tears mingled with Peter's. All this was like a love that suddenly came to me, the love I had been dreaming of. It is a love that transforms everything inside you and you ask yourself, *How could I live without this?*

I remember one time when I woke in the middle of the night from the disturbing snoring of my fellow patients. They had become quite deaf from streptomycin, and something went wrong in their respiratory organs. Their snoring sounded unnatural, rather as if they were weeping loudly. It was heart breaking and difficult to bear.

A street lamp burned in the darkness beyond the window, and snowflakes whirled in the cone of light. It was a swaying sea of light and darkness. Close to the window the snow dropped softly, wetly, touching the panes, while further away all flew up from the ground, whirled and vanished into the darkness. I suddenly realized that it was a theatre that played for me: white fireworks sparkling and soft snowflakes thrown in handfuls onto the windowpane. I was the sole spectator admiring this luxurious sight. The winter night spread its endless treasures in front of me to make me happy for a while.

Then I felt how the goodness of the world was enveloping me. I lay in a warm room and looked out of a window that someone had washed clean for me. I lay covered by a sheet that someone's hands had woven for me. No doubt, those who grew the cotton, who plucked it, who processed it and made threads, knew nothing of me, but their labors combined to make me warm. All people work for each other, and one can endlessly be glad of that.

I felt happy. I wanted to do something to please God. He, who woke me up to tell me that life was a real wonder, what could I do to make him glad—I, sick, alone, and ignorant? I thought that maybe my obedience would please him. *I'll go to the church and be baptized to be closer to him. But what church am I to go to? Granny Zhenia is from a Russian Orthodox family of a group called Old Believers, and her husband—my grandfather—was Lutheran. His mother—my great-grandmother—was Catholic. Papa was an atheist, and his parents were true Jews. So who am I?*

I decided to be baptized in the Orthodox Church. The

woman who prayed in the hospital restroom was Orthodox. She had shared her beloved church with me. "When the perishable has been clothed with the imperishable, and the mortal with immortality, then the saying that is written will come true: 'Death has been swallowed up in victory. Where, O death, is your victory? Where, O death, is your sting?'" (1 Cor. 15: 54-55)

All this I learned later, when books started to come miraculously into my hands, and when I met people of whom I could ask questions.

I had to go to the hospital to prepare for surgery on my hip joint. After that, I would remain a cripple for life. I decided to go and be baptized before the operation. A somewhat drunken priest baptized me. He yelled at everyone and gave orders right and left. It was cold, and I felt embarrassed each time a curious head poked over the folding screen that separated the baptistry from the remaining part of the church.

I put aside my crutches and stepped barefoot onto a damp gray rag. A draft swayed my long nightgown. I kept thinking of Mama. *Where is her poor soul? Can she see me?*

It was the beginning of an icy March, just about the time of her birthday. What an interesting coincidence; or was it a coincidence? Suddenly a sun ray flamed through a church window: summery, clear, and joyful. It fell over my frozen feet, as if covering them with a warm palm leaf. A calm was enthroned in my heart that I had never experienced before: a feeling of triumphant joy and clarity. The sacrament began, and our irritated priest started to calm down, grew kinder, and sobered up. And we who were there to be baptized, no longer annoyed him with our muddle-headedness.

He commanded me to come the next day for the Eucharist. I had no idea what that was, but I decided to obey.

Besides, I wanted to order a requiem mass for Mama. So on the next day I got into an icy tram once again, slipping on the ice as I dragged myself along the slick sidewalks. To go about the city in icy weather, when your sole support is a couple of crutches, isn't an easy task.

I came into the church. A common confession was going on, the church was overcrowded, and the priests could not talk privately with each person. I was disappointed to see it. I had read in Leskov's books that confession was a mystery. But there was no mystery in this church! Old women formed a most disorderly line where they hissed at one another, pushed and poked each other, and were restless as if they wanted to be through with it as soon as possible. Or perhaps they wanted to be the first ones to grab something. My spirits plummeted. I felt pity for Christ. Was this all he'd managed to achieve with his labors, his prayers, and his sufferings?

They let me, a cripple, go to the beginning of the queue, along with some ancient women. I stepped up to a priest with a stern and sorrowful expression on his face. He was an old man of medium height. His eyes startled me. Fatigued and faded, they had such a piercing look that I guessed this priest saw through everyone, but didn't get angry, didn't despise; rather pitied and loved everyone, even the bad. When I limped up to him, he straightened up and seemed to grow taller. With authority he stretched out his arm, as if separating me from the others. At this gesture the crowd fell back, and we remained alone by a little table with a crucifix and a Bible on a velvet cloth.

Looking earnestly into my eyes, the priest put his hands on my shoulders and said, "You're not alone anymore. Now the Heavenly Father will care for you. You're used to relying on yourself only. From now on, turn to him with every need. Tell me, do you talk to the photos of people you love when they have been long absent from you and you miss them? Well, look the same way at the icons and talk to the Father. Today you're born a second time. All your sins are cast off like a dirty old dress, thrown into the fire and burnt." Then he blessed me. He looked at me with sorrowful and tender understanding.

I was beyond myself with wonder. He knew nothing of me, nothing at all! I saw him that day for the first time in my life. But how can I explain to such a kind, responsive person that I was not being baptized to have my wishes granted by God. I thought it was not proper to bother God! *Am I really supposed to ask him for things?*

Very soon I made a discovery. It turns out that petitions can make the relationship closer, more intimate, while the hope that we are heard warms the soul. When a petition is answered, gratitude lights up the heart. Yes, one must ask! To remove all the obstacles, to make sure I have been heard. All this makes the asker who hopes for a response independent of circumstances, chance, fears, and the whims of other people. It leads to liberty!

After the service I remained in the church and waited for the old priest till he was free. I told him of Mama's death. I asked whether a funeral service could be read for her in church. He turned away and paused, his head bowed. Then he said that Mama wasn't guilty, because she was hunted down and driven to suicide. The sin had fallen on the one who had driven her to desperation, and more so, for her motives were to save her child and husband from her own hard destiny. That means she sacrificed herself for us.

The priest spread out a sheet of paper with a funeral prayer and a handful of soil on a little table, and we prayed together concerning my Mama. What a kind face he had! My tears dropped on the candle that was quietly burning right by my eyes, and my inner tension slowly released me, melting, vanishing. I welcomed hope.

Three days later I had a feeling in the early morning; something had happened or was about to happen and I had to go somewhere urgently. I tried to ignore the strange restlessness, but my fingers were all thumbs. I fretted and dashed about the room, and for some reason kept thinking of the face of the old priest as he prayed. His slight figure with hunched shoulders was all the time before me, and I thought of his eyes. Why were they so sorrowful? Perhaps he had seen so much human grief that his soul overflowed with the tears of others.

At last I could bear it no more. I took my crutches and trudged my way to the tram station. How slowly this tram crawled along the icy streets filled with dirty snowdrifts. I entered the church and at once saw a coffin that stood to the right of the entrance. Inside it lay someone with his face covered and dressed in priestly robes. Sallow old hands were peacefully folded on the chest.

"Who is that?" I asked.

"This is our Father Eugeny. You know him. He gave you the Eucharist, remember? He talked with you about something for a long time."

"But he was perfectly healthy! Can this really be him?"

"Oh, yes, it's him. He was reading a special prayer for a demon-possessed one. His heart failed. He was not too well that morning, but set off anyway. The mother of the demon-possessed boy entreated him and wept. Father Eugeny didn't spare himself, but spared and pitied others."

I walked up to the coffin and kissed the folded hands. I asked Father Eugeny to help the soul of my Mama, over there. I felt love bound us all together. If the dead can receive our living love, then it's clear why "for to God all are alive" (Luke 20:38). To God there are no dead people.

I have to add, much as it may seem incredible to some people, that very soon afterwards and most unexpectedly, I cast off my crutches. What's more, I no longer needed even a cane, because the tuberculosis of the hip joint simply vanished. The operation was no longer necessary.

But let me return to that woman in hospital who gave me a Gospel and advised me to be baptized in an Orthodox Church. She was a tiny woman with a severe curvature of the spine and paralyzed legs. She walked with crutches, and in fact walked on her arms. Her legs hung down as if made of rags. Her body weight was supported by her arms and shoulders, and her arms became strong and long. Her shoulders rose high, up to her chin.

Her name was Annie. A gentle child's smile always shone on her face—not childish, but a joyful, radiant smile. In Annie's life there were no reasons for joy. She developed tuberculosis of the spine in the war years, like I, when she was three. But there was no way for her to get into a hospital, and the tuberculosis ate down her spine in a very short time. She suffered from aches and muscle cramps. She often got boils in her armpits, and then it was a real torture to walk with her heavy crutches. Every touch of the crutches caused fiery pain. Annie's parents had died of tuberculosis when she was fourteen and her sister was six.

The girls were left in a 16-meter room in a communal apartment. People who lived in the same building wanted the room that Annie and her sister lived in. They advised Annie to move to a home for the disabled and put her sister into an orphanage. But Annie determined to raise her sister herself. She took work at the disabled workers cooperative.

She embroidered vests, and she got a small pension from the state. She brought up her sister, supported her studies in a technical school, and married her off.

Elderly women, with kerchiefs on their heads came quietly to visit Annie in the hospital. They slipped along the walls cautiously, as if they wanted to be taken for spirits or shadows. With disdain, other patients called them "churchists." They brought jam and fruit to Annie, and talked in whispers, leaning right to her pillow, and saw her off to the restroom. I knew that they prayed there together, when boils and pains tortured Annie too much.

Annie told me of a different Russia, fully unknown to me: the Russia of convents, of old monks, of holy springs and pilgrims wandering around the country in hope of finding Truth or a cure for their illnesses. It existed parallel to our usual life full of fights for apartments, struggles for getting food, books, jobs; full of visits to one's friends, of trips to the Russian South or the Baltic states; of squabbles and making up, of faithlessness or sickness. It was a different life, full of its own dramas and joys, and of different values. I was stunned. I strained to imagine Annie as a pilgrim traveling with crutches and a little sack on her hunchback, so weak she feared every draft and crack in the pavement.

One day, after we'd been discharged from the hospital, I walked down a street with Annie. The passersby and people in bus windows cast glances at her. A well-groomed, well-fed couple exited a shop. The smartly-dressed lady smelled of expensive perfume. Pedestrians stepped aside to let the couple pass. Reaching us, the lady nodded in Annie's direction and to her companion said without embarrassment: "Pray, tell me, why do such people inhabit this world? They only make you depressed. I know what I'd have done with them."

Annie lowered her head and didn't slow her pace. As before, she kept throwing forward the crutches, leaning briefly on her crooked legs which she dragged behind her like a mermaid's tail along the sidewalk and made the next throw. *Thump ... thump ...*

She whispered to me, "Don't respond! Take no notice of it. I'm used to it by now."

Miracles happened to Annie. Once she got lost in a strange city in an icy blizzard. She realized that she was about to fall and freeze to death. It was twilight and there was not a living soul nearby. She started to pray and cry, and suddenly someone took her by her shoulder and led her through the blizzard.

He brought her to a porch and said. "Knock on the door. They'll let you in."

She looked at her benefactor. He was an old man, austere and tender, and his face seemed familiar to her. He gave her a smile and disappeared into the blizzard.

She knocked at the door she'd been shown. The door opened. It turned out that it was the house of the cleaner of the local church. In the corner where the icons were displayed, over the table there hung a large icon of Saint Nicholas of Miry Likiskie, ornate with embroidered cloth and paper roses. Annie raised her eyes to the icon and said, "That's him! That's the old man who brought me to you."

NINETEEN

My baptism and all that followed afterwards were accompanied by major changes in my soul and life for which I can offer no rational explanation. The best way I can express my conversion is like this: I felt as if I had returned to my home and I was welcomed. It was as if welcomers hurried to me to express their joy, their love, to pour gifts over me, to hug me, to console me. It was like that, even though I didn't have a spiritual mentor. No one explained the way of Christ to me, nor were those I asked able to explain it.

The Christians I knew were incapable of answering the simplest theological questions. The faith of some was simply the love of God that was given to them, just like the ability to breathe or to see. For others, faith was somber and strict. Their religious feelings bore a pagan and Old Testament coloring. They had a fear that life is a chain of inevitable sins with misfortunes punishing every wrong step, every sinful thought, any unsanctioned sigh. There was a horror of death and judgment. They were filled with dread that one is unprotected from evil. Fear of inevitable, eternal suffering and fear of the Last Judgment were ever before them.

Joyful faith, loving faith, trusting faith, faith with a reverential awe and not with the horror of a slave scared to death, appealed to me a lot more. It came to me in a dark and troubled period of my life. It was like a window suddenly bursting open, and warmth, the blue of the sky, and all the voices and colors of the world flooded into my inner darkness and narrowness. I felt I met a look full of love, and a friendly hand was extended to me.

I wanted to have the answers to so many questions. I had been an innocent, suffering child, alone in a world of fear, blood, and war. It seemed so unjust. What was the reason for this pain, for this loneliness, for the looming future of crippled life and hopeless misery? Who saved me from the abyss? Why did he save me? For what reason did he love me? Why did he walk beside me, rescuing me again and again?

The answers to my lonely queries started to come ... in my dreams!

One of the dreams, I believe, was a testing dream given to me so that I could understand and get to know myself. It was so that I could clarify my inner beliefs. I think back on it as a significant turning point in my life.

> *I am bicycling across a pine forest, hot from the sun. There are sandy patches along the way. I jump off the bike and lead it by the handlebars, my feet gliding ankle-deep into the hot and prickly sand. Then I ride on, letting the forest wind blow over my face. The wind smells of hot pine sap.*
>
> *The bike bumps over the pine roots, which are sprawled across the trail. I pass through stripes of light and shade. Chill and heat alternately sweep over my shoulders.*
>
> *The pine wood is like an austere temple without adornments, only pillars and the play of light and shade. Light pours down from the dome, from an immense height. The light even stands like pillars*

between the tree trunks. The fragrance of dry needles and pine sap—a forest incense—fills every corner of the majestic temple.

The pillars step aside and I ride onto a clearing covered with incredibly tall wild grass.

A ramshackle log cabin stands in the center of the clearing. I lean my bike against a small mound next to the wall. A lizard is basking in the sun, with its little feet spread wide apart. Its round shining eyes watch me closely. I mount the porch. The stairs sag and creak under my steps. The grass sticking out from the cracks between the boards is still.

I open the door. It's lined with old, padded jackets. A worn-out oilcloth on top long ago had turned into loosely hanging shreds. I walk into the room. Inside there is nothing but an office-like bookcase, with its door hanging sadly on a solitary hinge.

Through a dusty window one can glimpse the forest and the clearing, but now they look as gray and cheerless as they might look in the last months of a hopeless autumn.

My Granny Zhenia steps out of a dark corner and looks at me with a smile. I rush to her, but suddenly notice that her face is split with a barely visible serpent-like crack, thin as a silk thread. For tiny fractions of a second the halves of the face burst apart along the crack and immediately join back again. I realize it was not Granny Zhenia. But I have no fear, I merely stop.

'Go to the bookcase,' says Granny's impostor.

I go.

'Do you see a book on the shelf?'

The dusty opening of the bookcase reveals a large, high-quality book that is lying on a dirty shelf. The book must have been valuable Moroccan leather and thick parchment pages, yellowed from age. What a beautiful cover, shiny with nice bronze clasps!

'Take the book and open it,' is the calm order with an undercurrent of latent triumph. Why is there a shade of triumph in the voice?

The huge book takes off and flies into my outstretched hands, opening as it comes. Its pages flip one after another with a stiff rustle, puffing ancient dust at me. They are covered with cryptic symbols.

'If you read aloud what's written in this page, all your childhood sufferings will vanish from your life. Your mistakes will be erased, so will be your restlessness and all the deeds that make you ashamed. You'll be freed from them, as you'll be freed from pain, fear, blood, from plaster and operations, from misery and loneliness. Read, only read this aloud, and you'll have a different past, a different fate; happy, full of joy, gifts, and luck,' the voice of Granny's double murmurs behind my shoulder.

A hot wave of temptation sweeps over me.

I conclude that I only have to want to read it, and the cryptic symbols will become understandable. My tongue would pronounce by itself all the combinations of ancient sounds even though they are now unknown to me.

At this point I suddenly feel that it is unacceptable. One mustn't change anything in one's past, one mustn't renounce anything.

But why can't I simply remove the suffering from my life? It's my life, is it not? Why do I need them, all these sufferings?

When I was a sick child, lonely, among strangers, when I screamed from pain, bit my hands, thrashed about in fever, buried deep into my fears—it was my life. I lived on pain, high fever, and fear. I was inside the suffering. As soon as it released me for a while, I dropped off to sleep, exhausted. But for adults it was hard to observe my pain. Now, grown-up myself, I understand what it is like to watch the torments of a child. Still, the pain of a lonely old man, of a betrayed girl, of a woman beaten by her husband, of a young man who fell into the hands of sadists, the horror and despair of a cancer patient dying in an empty apartment—are these any smaller than my childhood sufferings? Who can weigh them and compare? Should we feel more pity for one than for another?

Does the suffering purify? I know from my own experience: It pulls one down, it distorts, it disfigures and cripples. Then maybe it's the resistance to these distortions that is purifying? Maybe it's the victory over one's weakness that elevates one?

If so, I mustn't draw a line between my current self and my self of the past. I mustn't cancel out my victories that cost me so much, that were so hard to attain. I mustn't turn away from my defeats that made me understand so much.

I feel that it would be not only a painful, but a lethal choice. It would destine the lonely child in a stranger's cabin I had been then, to eternal suffering without hope for a change for the better, should I renounce it now. Perhaps, I'm one of those people who must gather their experiences and define their system of values through suffering and hardship.

Christ himself went through suffering to make each of us spiritually alive. Of his free will he took the hardest of crosses. He could have easily overcome the loneliness, the jeering, the execution itself. He didn't evade anything; he endured it all. He, who was without sin! Then what about me, with my load of sins, should I renounce my cross?

I suddenly see that one cannot extract any brick from the building of one's life. The entire building will collapse.

It takes only a moment for all this to dart through my mind, and I say to Granny's double, 'No, I take my cross.'

There is a short rumble inside the book in my hands, as if something exploded or a remote thunder rumbled far away. I return the book to the shelf. How difficult it is to do it! My hands feel for a second as if they are petrified. A little, gray cloud of dust flies into my face from the bookcase.

I turn to the one who pretends to be Granny Zhenia. Its face is now split into several parts, and each lives of itself. One corner of the mouth twists, the other is grinning. One eye looks piercingly, the other weeps. Then Granny's double burns with rage, like a red-hot iron. Now everything is lit by it as though by a blazing torch.

I find myself back on my bicycle in the pine forest temple. I pedal on and look at the iridescent pillars of sunlight between the tree trunks.

TWENTY

I wonder how I got into this world so full of life, motion, and sweet scents; into the sanctuary full of warmth, joy, and peace. I'm here, but I lost all my near and dear ones. What a strange path my life took.

Usually, when a man dies, he leaves his loved ones gradually, step by step. His habits and acts fade from their memory, his things vanish with time, getting lost or worn out. My dead relations, on the contrary, wove ever deeper and deeper into the fabric of my life. As I got older they took an increasingly-prominent place in my consciousness. The more I learned about them from their letters, diaries, notes, and pictures—the more I listened to the reminiscences of those who had known them—the more they filled me with life and new feeling.

And so it happens that my parents live with me, though physically they are no more. It is as if they are living, only in a different country, and might return at any minute. Our love gets stronger and stronger, our friendship is closer and closer, and we are very dear to each other.

A reproduction of the picture of Christ ("Image Made Without Hands") by a German painter, was found between the pages of Mama's diary. It's the face of a beautiful, suffering man left on a worn-out fabric. His eyes are closed, but somehow it seems he's looking straight into your soul.

When Mama was eighteen she wrote:

> *Christ is everywhere. The idea of Christ created hundreds of ages ago still has found no equal competitor. The things a normal man strives to achieve, the things he deems good, what he knows instinctively—that is nothing other than the image of Christ. I don't believe Christ ever existed physically. The idea of Christ is more marvelous than anything ever created by humankind during its entire existence. I don't understand how this idea could have been created so long ago, when even now it's impossible to grasp. The final collapse of religion is the victory of Christ, not his defeat. The idea must no longer be subjected to perversion and speculation. Superstition must fall, must be annihilated in the name of Christ. The man of the future is Christ. Not a man, but mankind. Christ is everywhere. ... Wide is the path of progress, the summit of the scientific.*

Here her writing ends.

What can one say to it?

Father also had faith in human progress and summits of science. All answers were to be found in scientific progress. These promising, icy pinnacles inspired and fed atheism, tinted by the destructive turbulences of the era.

In my youth, I kept thinking of the "country" where my parents are now. I didn't want to try to break into this country through the back door, turning to spiritualism and the occult. I looked at such practices with disgust and enmity, as did the women in the ward of my childhood. I knew that the mystery of the occult was to remain a mystery. I started to look for answers, instead, in the Bible. The Bible carries all the knowledge a man can accommodate without any destruction to himself and without breaking the laws of his nature. The Bible compiles the mystical experience of mankind. It mingles so naturally with the knowledge of life that one perceives it as a healthy and right approach to all questions of existence.

Papa wanted to tear Mama back from the claws of death. But he had no one and nothing to rely on. What would have happened if the followers of Fedorov, who deemed "future resurrection on the basis of the natural sciences" possible, had managed to bring back to life millions of dead men? Warriors would have gotten up, their hands clutching the rusted rot of their weapons, and they would have continued the fight, using their fists, rocks, and clubs—because their hatred, fear, pride, and self-interest would have been resurrected with them. Diseases and deformities would have risen from the graves, as well, forever inseparable from their victims. Many of the dead would have recoiled at the prospect of life, for they found in it no blessing, but only injustice and suffering. To suffer eternally—what an unbearable prospect! There would be no way one could avoid it. The kingdom of violence would have been resurrected with the people, for a resurrection like that wouldn't have transformed the resurrected internally—or for that matter, externally either.

I try to imagine what it would have been like if Papa had managed to bring Mama back to life. She would have found herself in the same hopeless situation: an exile with a lifelong stigma, no future, no way to build a future for herself or for her dear ones. How frightening! What future could she expect? The best possibility would still be war and exile. But the worst possible and most likely outcome would have been arrest, prison, and gulag.

Had she been a Christian, she would have had inner protection. All might have come to a different end. The avalanche of evil would have covered her anyway, but so much depends on the state you're in when the avalanche is speeding at you.

The Holy Scripture promises a resurrection of everyone, too. But this is a totally different resurrection! I read in the prophet Ezekiel of the resurrection of many people, whose bones covered the plain. The Lord himself put a hand on the prophet's shoulder and brought him to that vast plain, all covered with white bones, dried by the sun, washed by the rain. He told the prophet to command the bones to join again, and then to call for the breath of the four winds, from the four corners of the earth, to enter the ones who were lying on the plain. Ezekiel fulfilled the orders of the Lord, and the warriors who had decayed ages ago, came back to life on the battlefield, got up and ...

And these innumerable hosts, where will they go?

The Lord himself will take them to the Promised Land, to the quiet land with rivers whose waters are sweet as honey. Here cows stand knee-deep in the warm grass on the banks, fat and full of milk. The mist extends along the river valleys.

They will come into a different, transformed world, a world where the will of the Creator is restored, where nothing stands between God and man. There a river flows, mighty, clear as crystal—the river of life. It rolls in light-bearing waves along a wide street of the city built of precious stones, and on both sides of the river, right and left, there stand trees of life, and their leaves are meant for the healing of the peoples.

So it is written in Revelation 22. And so I believe.

Tamara Herbst (Marianna's mother) as a child. Mother and daughter looked so much alike!

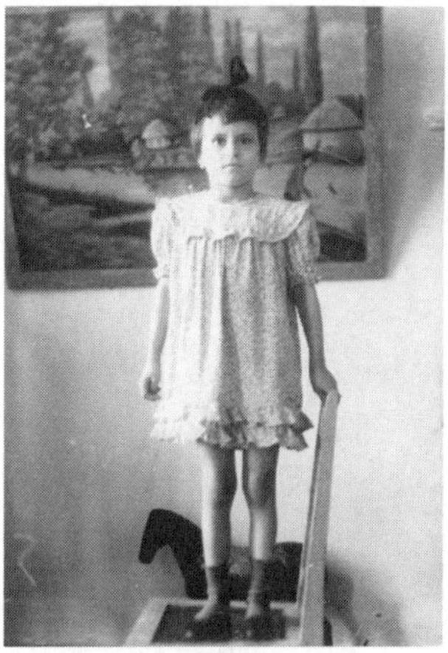

Marianna upon release from the sanatorium in 1947.

Tamara Herbst, 1937, just before exile.

Marianna as an adult.

Older siblings of Marianna's father, who along with another child was too small to pose for the photo. These are 8 of Granny Brina's 10 children. They were Jewish.

Aunt Leah,
Marianna's father's sister,
who found and saved the orphaned and ill Marianna, who had been abandoned by strangers during the war evacuation.
(1942)

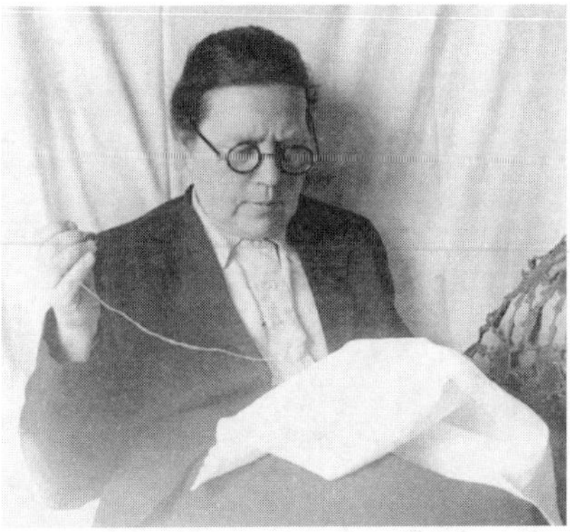

Aunt Elena, Marianna's father's aunt who played the piano and with whom Marianna spent summers before the war.

Marianna's father, Basil (called Bem) as a soldier in 1941.

Basil, who was an astronomer, giving a lecture at the planetarium in Moscow.

Granny Brina and Grampa Mark, 1940 (with two daughters and grandchildren).

Granny Zhenia,
Marianna's mother's
mother, and her
husband, Alfred Herbst.
He lived to age 26.
She was Russian,
he was German.

Marianna's mother, Tamara, as a child with her parents in Berlin.

Tamara with Zhenia, who was widowed by then.

Granny Zhenia in Moscow, 1957.

Marianna in her youth
as a university student.

A recent photo of Marianna as a volunteer at a Moscow mission, teaching street children about Jesus Christ.

About The Author

Marianna Vekhova is a graduate of Moscow State University, School of Journalism. She worked as an editor for a children's publishing house for five years, after which she wrote scripts for children's radio and television. She has published several children's books in Russian. She also did volunteer work with street children at a local mission for several years. In this capacity, she created a drama workshop and shared her faith in Jesus Christ.

Ms. Vekhova is now a freelance writer, creating religious publications for the Russian Orthodox Church youth movement. She resides in Moscow with her husband. She has a grown daughter, and grandchildren.